Careers for You Series

McGraw-Hill's

CAREERS FOR

PERSUASIVE TYPES

& Others Who Won't Take No for an Answer

JAN GOLDBERG

SECOND EDITION

New York   Chicago   San Francisco   Lisbon   London   Madrid   Mexico City
Milan   New Delhi   San Juan   Seoul   Singapore   Sydney   Toronto

Library of Congress Cataloging-in-Publication Data

Goldberg, Jan.
    Careers for persuasive types & others who won't take no for an answer / Jan
Goldberg — 2nd ed.
      p. cm. — (McGraw-Hill careers for you series)
      ISBN 0-07-147617-2 (alk. paper)
      1. Vocational guidance.   2. Oral communication.   3. Persuasion
(Psychology).   4. Negotiation in business.   I. Title.

HF5381.G56824 2007
331.702—dc22   2006028913

1 2 3 4 5 6 7 8 9 10 11 12 13 14 15   DOC/DOC   0 9 8 7

ISBN-13: 978-0-07-147617-1
ISBN-10:   0-07-147617-2

Contents

Acknowledgments

The author gratefully acknowledges the following individuals for their contributions:

- The numerous professionals who graciously agreed to be profiled in this book
- My dear husband, Larry, for his inspiration and vision
- My children—Sherri, Deborah, and Bruce—for their encouragement and love
- Family and close friends—Adrienne, Marty, Mindi, Cary, Michele, Paul, Michele, Alison, Steve, Marci, Steve, Brian, Steven, Jesse, Collin, Andrew, Bertha, Aunt Helen—for their faith and support
- Diana Catlin for her insights and input
- Blythe Camenson and Lillie Yvette Salinas for their continuing support

The editors would like to thank Josephine Scanlon for her work on this revision.

Introduction

....

By persuading others, we convince ourselves.

—Junius

Webster defines the word *persuade* in the following manner: induce belief in; convince. What personal qualities make someone persuasive? Are you the kind of person whom others find to be persuasive? Do you think you are a persuasive person? Take the following true-or-false quiz, and it just might provide some valuable insight into your personality.

Persuasiveness Quiz

1. I am able to think of several different ways to present a project or an idea.
2. I am usually able to make other people see a problem (or challenge) my way.
3. I enjoy new experiences.
4. Challenges excite me.
5. I trust my intuition.
6. I continue on with a project or idea even after most people have given up.
7. I find it easy to talk with strangers.
8. I avoid thinking in terms of success and failure.
9. I try to get to know as many people as possible in social situations.
10. Even in a new environment, I have no problem making contacts quickly.
11. People tend to remember me, even after only one contact.

12. I have a good memory for names, faces, and details.
13. I am an outgoing person.
14. I am able to think logically.
15. I am good at solving problems.
16. I am a good listener.
17. I am able to organize my thoughts effectively.
18. I am self-confident.
19. I am able to adjust my approach to the situation at hand.
20. I am a gregarious person.
21. I follow through on projects.
22. People like me.
23. I am goal-oriented.
24. I read profusely.
25. I strive for success, both for myself and for those with whom I interact.

If most of your responses were true, you may indeed be a persuasive person. If so, you might want to seriously consider exploring some of the careers highlighted in this book. All of them, particularly sales, advertising, marketing, public relations, fundraising, politics, law, and education, lend themselves to success for those individuals who have persuasive personalities.

One of our most well-known presidents had an interesting view on the concept of persuasion:

I sit here all day trying to persuade people to do the things they ought to have sense enough to do without my persuading them. That's all the powers of the president amount to.
—Harry S. Truman

CHAPTER ONE

Careers in Sales

*[A salesman is] an optimist who finds the world
full of promising potential.*
—Jerry Dashkin

The field of sales provides many opportunities for those with a talent for persuasion. Sales work encompasses a wide range of job settings, products, and services, as well as methods of selling. Here's a sample advertisement that captures some of the elements of a career in sales.

HELP WANTED: RETAIL SALES

If you enjoy art and design, work well with people, and are looking for an interesting and challenging full-time job, we have the ideal position in our art gallery. Your schedule will include Saturday hours from 10 A.M. until 6 P.M. and Sunday from noon until 5 P.M. Compensation will depend upon applicant's qualifications. If you are interested, please contact us immediately.

Sales careers can be broken into the following three primary categories:

- Retail
- Services
- Manufacturing and wholesale

Other areas that don't fit neatly into one of these three categories include insurance sales, real estate sales, and travel sales.

Retail Sales Workers

Millions of dollars are spent each day on all types of merchandise—everything from sweaters and books to food and furniture. Whether selling clothing, cosmetics, or automobiles, a sales worker's primary job is to interest customers in the merchandise. This can be accomplished by describing the product's features, demonstrating its use, showing various models and colors, and pointing out why products will benefit the customer or client.

Special knowledge and skills are needed for some jobs, particularly those that involve selling expensive and complex items. For example, workers who sell personal computers must be able to explain the features of various brands and models, the meaning of manufacturers' specifications, and the types of software that are available. In jobs selling standardized articles such as food, hardware, linens, and housewares, sales workers may often do little more than take payments and bag purchases.

Some retail sales workers also receive cash, check, and credit card payments; handle returns; and give change and receipts. Depending on the hours they work, they may have to open or close the cash register. This may include counting the money in the cash register; separating charge slips, coupons, and exchange vouchers; and making deposits at the cash office. Sales workers are often held responsible for the contents of the register, and in many organizations, repeated shortages are cause for dismissal.

In addition, sales workers may help stock shelves or racks, arrange for mailing or delivery of a purchase, mark price tags, take inventory, and prepare displays. Sales workers must be aware of the promotions their stores are sponsoring, as well as those that are being run by competitors. Also, they often must recognize possible security risks and know how to handle such situations.

Consumers often form their impressions of a store by its sales force. The retail industry is very competitive, and employers are increasingly stressing the importance of providing courteous and efficient service. For example, when a customer wants a product that is not available, the salesperson may place a special order or call another store to locate the item.

Job Settings

The largest employers of retail sales workers are department stores. Other types of employers include specialty shops, boutiques, independently owned stores, and large chain outlets, such as those selling hardware or office supplies.

Catalog and online sales are two large areas that provide additional avenues for those interested in venturing into sales as a career. In fact, the online sales market continues to broaden and deepen, with more products and services available online taking a bigger and bigger share of the total sales market.

Telemarketing is another huge industry. Everything can be sold by phone—from time-share vacations to telephone service to credit cards.

Qualifications and Training

Usually, there are no formal education requirements for this type of work. Employers look for candidates who enjoy working with people and have the tact and patience to deal with difficult customers. Among other desirable characteristics are an interest in sales, a neat appearance, and the ability to communicate clearly and effectively. Before hiring, some employers conduct background checks, especially for jobs involving high-priced items. Drug screening is also a common practice.

In most small stores, an experienced employee or the proprietor instructs newly hired sales workers in making out sales checks and operating the cash register. In larger stores, training programs are more formal and usually are conducted over several days.

As salespeople gain experience and seniority, they usually move to positions of greater responsibility and are given their choice of departments, which can mean moving to areas with potentially higher earnings and commissions. The highest earning potential is usually found selling big-ticket items, work that often requires the most knowledge of the product and the greatest talent for persuasion.

Although in the past, capable sales workers without a college degree could advance to management positions, large retail businesses today generally prefer to hire college graduates as management trainees, making a college education increasingly important. Despite this trend, capable employees without a degree should still be able to advance to administrative or supervisory work in large stores.

Opportunities for advancement vary in small stores. In some establishments, advancement is limited because one person, often the owner, does most of the managerial work. In others, however, some sales workers are promoted to assistant managers.

Retail selling experience may be an asset when applying for sales positions with larger retailers or in other industries, such as financial services, wholesale trade, or manufacturing.

Salaries

The starting salary for many part-time retail sales positions is the federal minimum wage. In some areas where employers have difficulty attracting and retaining workers, wages are much higher than the established minimum.

Compensation systems vary by type of establishment and merchandise sold. Some sales workers receive an hourly wage; others receive a commission or a combination of wages and commissions. Under a commission system, salespeople receive a percentage of the sales they make. These systems offer sales workers the opportunity to significantly increase their earnings, but sales workers may find their earnings depend on the ups and downs of the economy as well as their ability to sell the product.

Median hourly earnings of retail salespersons, including commissions, were $8.98 in 2004. The middle 50 percent earned between $7.46 and $12.22 an hour. The lowest 10 percent earned less than $6.38, and the highest 10 percent earned more than $17.85 an hour.

Median hourly earnings in the industries employing the largest numbers of retail salespersons were as follows:

Automobile dealers	$18.61
Building material and supplies dealers	$10.85
Department stores	$8.47
Other general merchandise stores	$8.36
Clothing stores	$8.17

In addition, nearly all sales workers are able to buy store merchandise at a discount, often from 10 to 40 percent below regular prices. In some cases, this privilege is extended to the employee's family as well.

Services Sales Representatives

Services sales representatives sell a wide variety of services. For example, sales representatives for data processing services firms sell complex services such as inventory control, payroll processing, sales analysis, and financial reporting systems. Hotel sales representatives contact government, business, and social groups to solicit convention and conference business for the hotel.

Sales representatives for temporary help services firms locate and acquire clients who will hire the firm's employees. Telephone services sales representatives visit commercial customers to review their telephone systems, analyze their communications needs, and recommend services such as installation of additional equipment. Other representatives sell automotive leasing, public utility, shipping, protective, and management consulting services.

Services sales representatives act as industry experts, consultants, and problem solvers when selling their firms' services. In some cases, the sales representative creates demand for the firm's services. A prospective client who is asked to consider buying a particular service may never have used, or even been aware of a need for, that service. For example, wholesalers persuaded to order a list of credit ratings to check their customers' credit prior to making sales may discover that the list could be used to solicit new business.

There are several different categories of services sales jobs:

- **Outside sales representatives** call on clients and prospects at their homes or offices. They may have an appointment, or they may practice cold calls, arriving without an appointment.
- **Inside sales representatives** work on their employers' premises, assisting individuals interested in the company's services.
- **Telemarketing sales representatives** sell exclusively over the telephone. They make large numbers of calls to prospects, attempting to sell company services themselves or to arrange appointments between the prospects and an outside sales representative.

Despite the diversity of services being sold, the jobs of all services sales representatives have much in common. All sales representatives must fully understand and be able to discuss the services their companies offer. Also, the procedures they follow are similar. Many sales representatives develop lists of prospective clients through telephone and business directories, asking business associates and customers for leads and calling on new clients as they cover their assigned territory. Some services sales representatives acquire clients who inquire about their companies' services. Some sales representatives deal exclusively with one, or a few, major clients.

Regardless of how they first meet the client, all representatives must explain how the services being offered can meet client needs. This often involves demonstrations of company services. Sales reps must answer questions about the nature and cost of the services and try to overcome objections in order to persuade potential customers to purchase the services. If they fail to make a sale on the first visit, they may follow up with more visits, letters, or phone calls. After closing a sale, representatives generally make follow-up calls or visits to check that the purchase meets the customer's needs and to determine whether additional services can be sold.

Because services sales representatives secure many of their new accounts through referrals, success hinges on developing a satisfied clientele who will continue to use the services and will recommend them to other potential customers. Like other types of sales jobs, a services sales representative's reputation is crucial to his or her success.

Services sales work varies with the kind of service sold. Selling highly technical services, such as communications systems or computer consulting services, involves complex and lengthy sales negotiations. In addition, sales of such complex services may require extensive after-sale support. In these situations, representatives may operate as part of a team of sales representatives and experts from other departments who provide valuable technical assistance. For example, those who sell data processing services might work with a systems engineer or computer scientist, and those who sell telephone services might receive technical assistance from a communications consultant. Teams enhance customer service and build strong long-term relationships with customers, resulting in increased sales.

Because of the length of time between the initial contact with a customer and the actual sale, representatives who sell complex technical services generally work with several customers simultaneously. For this reason, they must be well organized and efficient in scheduling their time.

Selling less complex services, such as exterminating or linen supply services, generally involves simpler and shorter sales negotiations. A sales representative's job may likewise vary with the size of the employer. Those working for large companies generally are more specialized and are assigned territorial boundaries, a specific line of services, and their own accounts. In smaller companies, sales representatives may have broader responsibilities in addition to their sales duties, such as administrative, marketing, or public relations.

Job Settings

Services sales representatives hold more than five hundred thousand jobs nationwide. More than half of these jobs are in firms providing business services, including computer and data processing; advertising; personnel supply; equipment rental and leasing; and mailing, reproduction, and stenographic services.

Other sales representatives work for firms that offer a wide range of services, such as business services (advertising, computer and data processing, personnel supply, mailing), engineering and management, amusement and recreation, automotive repair, membership organizations, hotels, motion pictures, health, and education.

Qualifications and Training

Many employers require services sales representatives to have a college degree, but requirements may vary depending on the industry a particular company represents. Employers who market advertising services seek individuals with a college degree in advertising or marketing or a master's degree in business administration; companies that market educational services prefer individuals with an advanced degree in marketing or a related field.

Many hotels seek graduates from college hotel administration programs, and companies that sell computer services and telephone systems prefer sales representatives with a background in computer science or engineering. College courses in business, economics, communications, and marketing are helpful in obtaining other jobs as services sales representatives.

Some employers hire experienced, high-performing sales representatives who have only a high school diploma. This is particularly true for those who sell nontechnical services, such as exterminating, laundry, or funeral services.

Many firms conduct intensive training programs for their sales representatives. A sound training program covers the history of the business; origin, development, and uses of the service; effective prospecting methods; presentation of the service; answering customer objections; creating customer demand; closing a sale; writing an order; company policies; and using technical support personnel.

Sales representatives also may attend seminars on a wide range of subjects given by in-house or outside training institutions. These sessions acquaint employees with new services and products, help them maintain and update their sales techniques, and may include motivational or sensitivity training to make sales representatives more effective in dealing with people. Sales staffs generally receive training in the use of computers and communications technology in order to increase their productivity.

In order to be successful, sales representatives should have pleasant, outgoing personalities and good rapport with people. They must be highly motivated, well organized, and efficient.

Good grooming and a neat appearance are essential, as are self-confidence, reliability, and the ability to communicate effectively. Sales representatives should be self-starters who have the ability to work under pressure to meet sales goals.

Sales representatives who have good sales records and leadership ability may advance to supervisory and managerial positions. Frequent contact with businesspeople in other firms provides sales workers with leads about job openings, enhancing advancement opportunities.

Salaries

The average yearly income for entry-level sales workers is about $36,000, ranging up to $63,000 for senior sales staff. Earnings of experienced sales representatives depend on performance. Successful sales representatives who establish a strong customer base can sometimes earn more than their managers. Some sales representatives earn well over $100,000 a year.

Sales representatives work on different types of compensation plans. Some receive a straight salary; others are paid solely on commission, receiving a percentage of the dollar value of their sales. Most firms use a combination of salary and commissions.

Some services sales representatives receive a base salary plus incentive pay that adds 50 to 70 percent to the base salary. In addition to the same benefits package received by other employees of the firm, outside sales representatives have expense accounts to cover meals and travel, and some drive a company car. Many employers offer bonuses, including vacation time, trips, and prizes, for sales that exceed company quotas.

Earnings of representatives who sell technical services generally are higher than earnings of those who sell nontechnical services. In spite of all the perks, with fluctuating economic conditions and consumer and business expectations, earnings may vary widely from year to year.

Manufacturers' and Wholesale Sales Representatives

Articles of clothing, books, and computers are among the thousands of products bought and sold each day, and manufacturers' and wholesale sales representatives play an important role in this process. While retail sales workers sell products directly to customers, manufacturers' representatives market company products to other manufacturers, wholesale and retail establishments, government agencies, and institutions. Regardless of the kinds of products they sell, the primary duties of these sales representatives are to interest wholesale and retail buyers and purchasing agents in their merchandise and to ensure that any questions or concerns of current clients are addressed. Sales representatives also provide advice to clients on how to increase sales.

Job titles in this field differ depending on the employment setting. Many of those representing manufacturers are referred to as manufacturers' representatives, and those employed by wholesalers generally are called sales representatives. Representatives who sell technical products, for both manufacturers and wholesalers, are usually called industrial sales workers or sales engineers. Rather than working directly for a firm, some manufacturers' agents are self-employed, contracting their services to all types of companies.

Manufacturers' and wholesale sales representatives spend much of their time traveling to and visiting with prospective buyers and current clients. During sales calls, they discuss the customers' needs and suggest how their products or services can meet those needs. They may show samples or catalogs that describe items their companies stock and inform customers about prices, availability, and how their products can save money and improve productivity. They also take orders and resolve any problems or complaints with the products and services.

These sales representatives have additional duties as well. For example, sales engineers, who are among the most highly trained sales workers, typically sell products that require technical expertise to install and use. They may also need to familiarize clients with support products, such as material-handling equipment, numerical-control machinery, and computer systems. Sales engineers also provide follow-up services, keeping close contact with clients to ensure that they renew their contracts. Sales engineers may also work with engineers in their own companies, customizing products to meet special customer needs.

Increasingly, sales representatives who lack technical expertise work on a team with a technical expert. For example, sales representatives make the preliminary contacts with customers, introduce the products, and close the sales. However, technically trained representatives attend the sales presentations to explain technical issues and answer questions and concerns. In this way, the sales representative is able to spend more time maintaining and soliciting accounts and less time gaining technical knowledge.

Obtaining new accounts is an important part of the job. Sales representatives follow leads from other clients, from advertisements in trade journals, and from participation in trade shows and conferences. At times, they make unannounced visits to potential clients. In addition, they may spend a lot of time meeting with and entertaining prospective clients during evenings and weekends.

Sales representatives also analyze sales statistics, prepare reports, and handle administrative duties, such as filing their expense account reports, scheduling appointments, and making travel plans. They study literature about new and existing products and monitor the sales, prices, and products of their competitors. Supervisors track the daily activities of sales reps—where they have been, who they have seen, and what they have sold.

Some manufacturers' and wholesale sales representatives have large territories and do considerable traveling. Because a sales region may cover several states, they may be away from home for several days or weeks at a time. Others work near their home bases and do most of their traveling by automobile. Because of the nature of the work and the amount of travel, sales representatives typically work more than forty hours per week.

Qualifications and Training

The background needed for sales jobs varies by product line and market. As the number of college graduates has increased and the job requirements have become more technical and analytical, most firms have placed a greater emphasis on a strong educational background. Nevertheless, many employers still hire individuals with previous sales experience who do not have a college degree. In fact, for some consumer products, an individual's sales ability, personality, and familiarity with brands are more important than a degree.

On the other hand, firms selling industrial products often require degrees in science or engineering in addition to some sales experience. In general, companies are looking for the best and brightest individuals who have the personal characteristics and desire necessary to sell.

Many companies have formal training programs for beginning sales representatives that last up to two years. However, most businesses are accelerating these programs to reduce costs and to expedite the return from training. In some programs, trainees rotate among jobs in plants and offices to learn all phases of production, installation, and distribution of the products. In others, trainees may take formal classroom instruction at the plant, followed by on-the-job training under the supervision of a field sales manager.

In some firms, new workers are trained by accompanying more experienced workers on sales calls. As they gain familiarity with the firm's products and clients, they are given increasing responsibility until they are eventually assigned their own territories. As businesses experience greater competition, increased pressure is placed upon sales representatives to produce faster.

Manufacturers' and wholesale sales representatives must stay abreast of new merchandise and the changing needs of their customers. Sales representatives should enjoy traveling because much of their time is spent visiting current and prospective clients. They may attend trade shows where new products are displayed or conferences and conventions where they meet with other sales representatives and clients to discuss new product developments. In addition, many companies sponsor meetings for the entire sales force to discuss sales performance, product development, and profitability.

Salaries

Compensation methods vary significantly by the type of firm and the products sold. However, most employers use a combination of salary and commission or salary plus bonus. Commissions are usually based on the amount of sales, whereas bonuses may depend on individual performance, on the performance of all sales workers in the group or district, or on the company's overall performance.

Median annual earnings of full-time manufacturers' and wholesale sales representatives average between $45,000 and $58,000, although some might start as low as $24,000 and others earn well over $100,000. Earnings vary by experience and the type of goods or services sold.

Manufacturers' and wholesale sales representatives are generally split into two categories, and those who sell technical and scientific products tend to earn more than those who sell nontechnical and nonscientific products. According to the *Occupational Outlook Handbook*, median annual earnings in 2004 in the industries employing the largest numbers of sales representatives selling technical and scientific products were as follows:

Computer systems design and related services $70,220
Wholesale electronic markets and agents
    and brokers $65,990
Drugs and druggists' sundries merchant
    wholesalers $60,130
Professional and commercial equipment
    and supplies merchant wholesalers $59,080
Electrical and electronic goods merchant
    wholesalers $52,870

Median annual earnings in the industries employing the largest numbers of sales representatives dealing in nontechnical and nonscientific products were as follows:

Wholesale electronic markets and agents
    and brokers $50,680
Machinery, equipment, and supplies
    merchant wholesalers $46,030
Professional and commercial equipment
    and supplies merchant wholesalers $45,320
Grocery and related product wholesalers $44,210
Miscellaneous nondurable goods
    merchant wholesalers $40,240

In addition to their earnings, sales representatives are usually reimbursed for expenses, including transportation costs, meals, hotels, and entertaining customers. They often receive benefits such as health and life insurance, a pension plan, vacation and sick leave, personal use of a company car, and frequent flyer mileage. Some companies offer additional incentives, such as free vacation trips or gifts for outstanding performance.

Unlike sales representatives working directly for a manufacturer or wholesaler, manufacturers' agents work strictly on commission.

Depending on the types of products they sell, their levels of experience in the field, and the number of clients they have, their earnings can be significantly higher or lower than for those working in direct sales. In addition, because manufacturers' agents are self-employed, they must pay their own travel and entertainment expenses and their own benefits, which can be significant costs. Frequently, promotion takes the form of an assignment to a larger account or territory where commissions are likely to be greater.

Experienced sales representatives may move into jobs training new employees on selling techniques and company policies and procedures. Those who have good sales records and leadership abilities may advance to sales supervisors or district managers. Others find opportunities in buying, purchasing, advertising, or marketing research. For many sales representativess, the end goal is to climb the ladder in sales and transfer into marketing.

Insurance Sales

Most people have their first contact with an insurance company through an insurance sales agent. These agents help individuals, families, and businesses select insurance policies that provide the best protection for their lives, health, and property. Agents prepare reports, maintain records, seek out new clients, and, in the event of a loss, help policyholders settle their insurance claims. Increasingly, some are also offering their clients financial analysis or advice on ways the clients can minimize risk.

Insurance sales agents sell one or more types of insurance, such as property and casualty, life, health, disability, and long-term care. Property and casualty insurance agents sell policies that protect individuals and businesses from financial loss resulting from automobile accidents, fire, theft, storms, and other events that can damage property. For businesses, property and casualty insurance can also cover injured workers' compensation, product liability claims, or medical malpractice claims. Life insurance agents specialize in selling policies that pay beneficiaries when a policy-holder dies, as well as annuities that promise a retirement income. Health insurance agents sell policies that cover the costs of medical care and loss of income due to illness or injury. They also may sell dental insurance and short-term and long-term disability insurance policies.

An increasing number of insurance sales agents offer comprehensive financial planning services to their clients, such as retirement planning, estate planning, or assistance in setting up pension plans for businesses. As a result, many insurance agents are involved in cross-selling or total account development. Besides offering insurance, these agents may become licensed to sell mutual funds, variable annuities, and other securities. This practice is most common with life insurance agents who already sell annuities; however, property and casualty agents also sell financial products.

Technology has greatly affected the insurance agency, making it much more efficient and giving agents the ability to take on more clients. Agents' computers are now linked directly to insurance carriers via the Internet, making the tasks of obtaining price quotes and processing applications and service requests faster and easier. Computers also allow agents to be better informed about new products that the insurance carriers may be offering.

Because insurance sales agents also obtain many new accounts through referrals, it is important that they maintain regular contact with their clients to ensure that the clients' financial needs are being met. Developing a satisfied clientele that will recommend an agent's services to other potential customers is a key to success in this field.

Qualifications and Training

Most companies and independent agencies prefer to hire college graduates as insurance sales agents, especially those who have majored in business or economics. High school graduates are occasionally hired if they have proven sales ability or have been successful in other types of work. In fact, many entrants to insurance sales agent jobs transfer from other occupations. In selling commercial insurance, technical experience in a particular field can help sell policies to those in the same profession. As a result, new agents tend to be older than entrants in other occupations.

College training may help agents grasp the technical aspects of insurance policies and the fundamentals and procedures of selling insurance. Many colleges and universities offer courses in insurance, and a few schools offer a bachelor's degree in the field. College courses in finance, mathematics, accounting, economics, business law, marketing, and business administration enable insurance sales agents to understand how social and economic conditions relate to the insurance industry. Courses in psychology, sociology, and public speaking can prove useful in improving sales techniques. Familiarity with computers and popular software packages has become very important because computers provide instantaneous information on a wide variety of financial products and greatly improve agents' efficiency.

Insurance sales agents must be licensed by the state where they plan to work. Separate licenses are required for agents to sell life and health insurance and property and casualty insurance. In most states, licenses are issued only to applicants who complete specified prelicensing courses and who pass state examinations covering insurance fundamentals and state insurance laws. The insurance industry is increasingly moving toward uniform state licensing standards and reciprocal licensing, allowing agents who earn a license in one state to become licensed in other states upon passing the appropriate courses and examination.

A number of organizations offer professional designation programs that certify an agent's expertise in specialties such as life, health, and property and casualty insurance, as well as financial consulting. For example, the National Alliance for Education and Research offers a wide variety of courses in health, life, and property and casualty insurance for independent insurance agents. These voluntary programs assure clients and employers that an agent has a thorough understanding of the relevant specialty. Agents are usually required to complete a specified number of hours of continuing education to retain the certification.

Given the diversity of financial products sold by insurance agents today, employers are also placing greater emphasis on continuing professional education. It is important for agents to keep current on issues concerning their clients. Changes in tax laws, government benefits programs, and other state and federal regulations can affect the insurance needs of clients and the way agents conduct business. Agents can enhance their selling skills and broaden their knowledge of insurance and other financial services by taking college and university courses and by attending institutes, conferences, and seminars sponsored by insurance organizations. Most state licensing authorities also have mandatory continuing education requirements focusing on insurance laws, consumer protection, and the technical details of various insurance policies.

Insurance sales agents should be flexible, enthusiastic, confident, disciplined, hard working, and willing to solve problems. They should communicate effectively and inspire customer confidence. Because they usually work without supervision, sales agents must be able to plan their time well and have the initiative to locate new clients. An insurance sales agent who shows ability and leadership may become a sales manager in a local office. A few advance to agency superintendent or executive positions. However, many who have built up a good clientele prefer to remain in sales work. Some agents, particularly in the property and casualty field, establish their own independent agencies or brokerage firms.

Salaries

Many independent agents are paid by commission only, whereas sales workers who are employees of an agency or an insurance carrier may be paid in one of three ways—salary only, salary plus commission, or salary plus bonus. In general, commissions are the most common form of compensation, especially for experienced agents. The amount of the commission depends on the type and amount of insurance sold and on whether the transaction is a new policy or a renewal. Bonuses usually are awarded when agents meet their sales goals or when an agency meets its profit goals. Some agents involved with financial planning receive a fee for their services, rather than a commission.

The median annual earnings of insurance sales agents were $41,720 in 2004. The middle 50 percent earned between $29,980 and $66,160. The lowest 10 percent had earnings of $23,170 or less, while the highest 10 percent earned more than $108,800. Median annual earnings in the two industries employing the largest number of insurance sales agents were $42,010 for insurance carriers and $41,840 for agencies, brokerages, and other insurance-related activities.

Company-paid benefits to insurance sales agents usually include continuing education, training to qualify for licensing, group insurance plans, office space, and clerical support services. Some companies also may pay for automobile and transportation expenses, attendance at conventions and meetings, promotion and marketing expenses, and retirement plans. Independent agents working for insurance agencies receive fewer benefits, but their commissions may be higher to help them pay for marketing and other expenses.

Real Estate Sales

Buying or selling a home or an investment property is not only one of the most important financial events in peoples' lives, it's one of the most complex transactions as well. As a result, people generally seek the help of real estate agents or brokers to complete these transactions.

Real estate agents and brokers need to have a thorough knowledge of the housing market in their communities. They must understand which neighborhoods best fit their clients' needs and budgets. They have to be familiar with local zoning and tax laws and know where to obtain financing. Agents and brokers also negotiate price between buyers and sellers.

Brokers

Brokers are independent businesspeople who sell real estate owned by others; they also may rent or manage properties for a fee. When selling real estate, brokers arrange for title searches and for meetings between buyers and sellers during which the details of the transactions are agreed upon and the new owners take possession of the property. A broker may help the prospective buyer to arrange favorable financing from a lender; often, this makes the difference between success and failure in closing a sale.

In some cases, brokers and agents assume primary responsibility for closing sales; in others, closings are handled by lawyers or lenders. Brokers supervise agents who may have many of the same job duties. Brokers also supervise their own offices, advertise properties, and handle other business matters. Some combine other types of work, such as selling insurance or practicing law, with their real estate business.

Agents

Real estate agents usually are independent sales workers who provide their services to a licensed broker on a contract basis. In return, the broker pays the agent a portion of the commission earned from the agent's sale of the property. Brokers provide office space, but agents generally furnish their own automobiles.

Responsibilities of Real Estate Professionals

When working with customers in real estate, the most important thing an agent does is to listen to their needs. It is not uncommon for clients to describe a dream home that is actually more expensive than they can afford. The agent's job begins with helping the clients to determine their priorities. Do they really need four bedrooms, for example, or will three do? Do they want one story or two? Do they need a room to serve as an office?

At this point, the agent or broker consults a mortgage broker to determine the clients' financial situation. This prequalification phase is very important because it tells the agent and clients how expensive a property they can afford.

Next the agent searches databases to find properties in the clients' price range. It is important for the agent to be well aware of the customers' needs and desires, so that time is not wasted in showing properties that the clients are not interested in.

Then, the house hunting begins. Agents spend a lot of time showing homes to prospective buyers. Once a home has been found and the contract has been signed by both parties, the broker or agent must ensure that all special terms of the contract are met before the closing date. For example, if the seller has agreed to a home inspection or termite and radon inspections, the agent must make sure that they are done. Sometimes these inspections reveal needed repairs; if the seller has agreed to any repairs, the broker or agent must see to it that repairs are completed satisfactorily before the sale can close.

Because brokers and agents must have properties to sell, they spend a significant amount of time obtaining listings (owner agreements to place properties for sale with the firm). They spend time on the telephone exploring leads gathered from various sources, including personal contacts. When listing properties for sale, agents and brokers make comparisons with similar properties that have been sold recently to determine fair price.

Most real estate agents and brokers sell residential property. A few, usually those from large firms or specialized small firms, sell commercial, industrial, agricultural, or other types of real estate.

Each specialty requires knowledge of that particular kind of property and clientele.

Although real estate agents and brokers usually work in offices, their time is primarily spent showing properties to customers, analyzing properties for sale, meeting with prospective clients, researching the state of the market, inspecting properties for appraisal, and performing a wide range of other duties.

Qualifications and Training

Real estate agents and brokers must be licensed in every state and the District of Columbia. Prospective agents must be high school graduates, be at least eighteen years old, and pass a written test that includes questions on basic real estate transactions and laws affecting the sale of property. The exam for brokers is more comprehensive than that for agents. Most states require candidates for the general sales license to complete between thirty and ninety hours of classroom instruction. Candidates for a broker's license need between sixty and ninety hours of formal training and usually one to three years of experience selling real estate. Some states waive the experience requirements for the broker's license for applicants who have a bachelor's degree in real estate.

State licenses typically must be renewed every one or two years; usually, no examination needs to be taken. However, many states require continuing education for license renewals. Exact licensing requirements are available from the real estate licensing commission of each state.

As real estate transactions have become more legally complex, many firms have turned to college graduates to fill positions. College courses in real estate, finance, business administration, statistics, economics, law, and English are helpful. For those who intend to start their own companies, business courses such as marketing and accounting are as significant as courses in real estate or finance.

Many firms offer formal training programs for both beginners and experienced agents. Larger firms usually offer more extensive programs than smaller firms. More than a thousand universities, colleges, and community colleges offer courses in real estate. At some, a student can earn an associate's or bachelor's degree with a major in real estate; several offer advanced degrees. Many local real estate associations that are members of the National Association of Realtors sponsor courses covering the fundamentals and legal aspects of the field. Advanced courses in mortgage financing, property development and management, and other subjects also are available.

Advancement opportunities for agents may take the form of higher rates of commission. As agents gain knowledge and expertise, they become more efficient in closing a greater number of transactions and increase their earnings. In many large firms, experienced agents can advance to sales manager or general manager. Those who have received a broker's license may open their own offices. Others with experience and training in estimating property value may become real estate appraisers, and people familiar with operating and maintaining rental properties may become property managers. Experienced agents and brokers with a thorough knowledge of business conditions and property values in their localities may enter mortgage financing or real estate investment counseling.

In this highly interactive and competitive field, personality traits are as important as academic background. Brokers look for agents who possess a pleasant personality, are honest, and present a neat appearance. Maturity, good judgment, trustworthiness, and enthusiasm for the job are required in order to encourage prospective customers in this highly competitive field. Agents should be well organized; be detail oriented; and have a good memory for names, faces, and business particulars.

Agents also have to be very careful when dealing with new clients who are strangers. This is especially true for female realtors.

Brokers often encourage their agents to work in pairs if possible and to always arrange the first meeting with the client to take place at the office, not at the property. Another precaution is to have clients follow in their own cars rather than ride with the agent.

Most every agent has experienced showing dozens of properties to a client without making a sale. While this is frustrating, it can be seen as an opportunity for an agent to gain additional knowledge about available properties.

Agents and brokers often work more than a standard forty-hour week. They usually work evenings and weekends and are always on call to suit the needs of clients. Business is often slower during the winter season. Although the hours are long and frequently irregular, most agents and brokers have the freedom to determine their own schedules. Consequently, they can arrange their work so that they can have time off when they want it.

Training for Real Estate Agents in Canada. According to the Canadian Real Estate Association, education and licensing requirements for jobs in the real estate industry are established by the individual provinces. Aspiring agents and brokers should check the requirements of the province in which they intend to sell real estate.

In most provinces, educational requirements must be met before one can enter the field. A period of supervised practical training, sometimes called articling, may also be required before a worker can be registered as a real estate professional.

Colleges and universities offer a variety of real estate or related courses. At many of these colleges, students can specialize in a program that leads to a bachelor's degree in real estate. Some universities offer graduate-level courses. Continuing education is also required in many provinces so that real estate professionals can stay current on the issues that affect the industry.

Provincial licensing is required throughout the country. Although licensing requirements vary, all provinces and territories require prospective salespeople and brokers to pass a written exam.

Salaries

Commissions on sales are the main source of earnings of real estate agents and brokers. The rate of commission varies according to whatever the agent and broker agree on, the type of property, and its value. The percentage paid on the sale of farm and commercial properties or unimproved land is typically higher than the percentage paid for selling a home.

Commissions may be divided among several agents and brokers. When a property is sold, the broker or agent who obtained the listing usually shares the commission with the broker or agent who made the sale and with the firms that employ each of them. Although an agent's share varies greatly from one firm to another, often it is about half of the total amount received by the firm. Agents who both list and sell properties are able to maximize their commissions.

The median annual earnings of salaried real estate sales agents, including commissions, were $35,670 in 2004. The middle 50 percent earned between $23,500 and $58,110 a year. The lowest 10 percent earned less than $17,600, and the highest 10 percent earned more than $92,770. The industries that employed the highest numbers of real estate agents were residential building construction, offices of real estate agents and brokers, activities related to real estate, and companies that lease real estate.

Median annual earnings of salaried real estate brokers, including commission, were $58,720 in 2004. The middle 50 percent earned between $33,480 and $99,820 a year. Median annual earning of real estate brokers were $61,550 in offices of real estate agents and brokers and $44,920 in activities related to real estate.

Income usually increases as agents gain experience, but individual motivation, economic conditions, and the type and location of properties sold also affect earnings. Sales workers who are active in community organizations and in local real estate associations can broaden their contacts and increase their earnings. A beginner's earnings often are irregular because a few weeks or even months may go by without making a sale. Although some brokers allow an agent to draw against future earnings from a special account, the practice is not common with new employees. The beginner, therefore, should have enough money to live for about six months or until commissions increase.

Travel Sales

Of all the industries worldwide, travel and tourism continue to grow at an astounding rate. In fact, according to the Travel Works for America Council, the travel industry is the second largest employer in the United States after health services. Nearly everyone tries to take at least one vacation every year, and many people travel frequently on business. Some people travel for education or for a special honeymoon or anniversary trip.

Constantly changing airfares and schedules, thousands of available vacation packages, and a vast amount of travel information on the Internet can make travel planning frustrating and time-consuming. To sort out the many travel options, tourists and businesspeople often turn to travel agents, who assess their needs and help them make the best possible travel arrangements. Also, many major cruise lines, resorts, and specialty travel groups use travel agents to promote their services to millions of people every year.

In general, travel agents give advice on destinations and make arrangements for transportation, hotel accommodations, car rentals, tours, and recreation. They may also advise on weather conditions, restaurants, tourist attractions, and a wide range of recreational activities.

For international travel, agents also provide information on customs regulations, required papers (passports, visas, and certificates of vaccination), and currency exchange rates.

Travel agents consult a variety of published and computer-based sources for information on departure and arrival times, fares, and hotel accommodations and ratings. They may visit hotels, resorts, and restaurants to evaluate comfort, cleanliness, and quality of food and service so that they can base recommendations on their own travel experiences.

Travel agents also promote their services, using telemarketing, direct mail, and the Internet. They make presentations to social and special-interest groups, arrange advertising displays, and suggest company-sponsored trips to business managers. Depending on the size of the travel agency, an agent may specialize by type of travel, such as leisure or business, or destination, such as Europe or Africa.

Travel agents spend most of their time behind a desk conferring with clients, completing paperwork, contacting airlines and hotels for travel arrangements, and promoting group tours. During vacation seasons and holiday periods, they may be under a great deal of pressure.

Many agents, especially those who are self-employed, frequently work long hours. With advanced computer systems and telecommunication networks, some travel agents are able to work at home.

Qualifications and Training

The minimum requirement for working as a travel agent is a high school diploma or equivalent. Technology and computerization have increased the training needs, however, and many employers prefer applicants with more education, such as a postsecondary vocational award.

Many vocational schools offer full-time travel agent programs that last several months, as well as evening and weekend programs. Travel agent courses also are offered in public adult education programs and in community and four-year colleges. A few colleges offer bachelor's or master's degrees in travel and tourism.

Although few college courses relate directly to travel or tourism, a college education often shows employers an applicant's background in fields such as computer science, geography, communication, foreign languages, and world history. Courses in accounting and business management also are important, especially for those who expect to manage or start their own travel agencies.

The American Society of Travel Agents offers a correspondence course that provides a basic understanding of the travel industry. Travel agencies also provide on-the-job training for their employees, mainly in the form of computer instruction. All employers require computer skills of workers whose jobs involve the operation of airline and centralized reservations systems.

The abundance of travel information available through the Internet has resulted in a more informed customer who wants to deal with an expert when planning a trip. For this reason, continuing education is very important to the travel agent. Experienced agents can take advanced self-study or group-study courses from the Travel Institute, leading to the Certified Travel Counselor designation. The Travel Institute also offers marketing and sales skills development programs and destination specialist programs, which provide detailed knowledge of regions such as North America, Western Europe, the Caribbean, and the Pacific Rim. With the trend toward more specialization, these and other destination specialist courses are increasingly important.

Personal travel experience or experience as an airline reservation agent is an asset because knowledge about a city or foreign country often helps influence a client's travel plans. Patience and the ability to gain the confidence of clients also are useful qualities. Travel agents must be well organized, accurate, and meticulous to compile information from various sources and plan and organize their clients' travel itineraries. Also, agents who specialize in business travel must work quickly and efficiently because business travel often must be arranged on short notice. In addition to computer skills, good writing and interpersonal and sales skills are also important.

Some employees start as reservation clerks or receptionists in travel agencies. With experience and some formal training, they can take on greater responsibilities and eventually assume travel agent duties. In agencies with many offices, travel agents may advance to office manager or to other managerial positions.

Those who start their own agencies generally have had experience in an established agency. Before they can receive commissions, these agents usually must gain formal approval from suppliers or corporations, such as airlines, cruise lines, or rail lines. For example, the Airlines Reporting Corporation and the International Airlines Travel Agency Network are the approving bodies for airlines. To gain approval, an agency must be financially sound and employ at least one experienced manager or travel agent.

There are no federal licensing requirements for travel agents, although in 2004 thirteen states required some form of registration or certification of retail sellers of travel services. More information may be obtained by contacting the attorney general or Department of Commerce in each state.

Salaries

Experience, sales ability, and the size and location of the agency determine the salary of a travel agent. Median annual earnings of travel agents were $27,640 in 2004. The middle 50 percent earned between $21,600 and $35,070. The lowest 10 percent earned less than $17,180, while the top 10 percent earned more than $44,090. Median earnings for travel agents employed in the travel arrangement and reservation services industry were $27,490.

Salaried agents usually enjoy standard employer-paid benefits that self-employed agents must provide for themselves. When traveling for personal reasons, agents usually get reduced rates for transportation and accommodations. In addition, agents sometimes take "familiarization" trips, at lower cost or no cost to themselves, to learn about various vacation sites. These benefits attract many people to this occupation.

Earnings of travel agents who own their agencies depend primarily on commissions from travel-related bookings and service fees they charge clients. Often it takes time to acquire a sufficient number of clients to have adequate earnings, so it is not unusual for new self-employed agents to have low earnings. Established agents may have lower earnings during economic downturns.

Words from the Pros

Five sales professionals have shared their experiences for readers of this book. Read on to see whether the following accounts interest your persuasive side.

Marty Gorelick, Computer Hardware Sales Professional

Marty Gorelick has a bachelor of arts degree from Long Island University in Brooklyn, New York, and more than a dozen years of experience in computer hardware sales. He has attended seminars sponsored by all of the major computer manufacturers: IBM, HP/Compaq, Sony, Apple, and NEC. He is account manager for county government sales at GE Capital IT Solutions in Miami, Florida, where he services Metro-Dade, Broward, and Pasco counties, plus all cities, towns, and villages within these counties.

"The computer industry is constantly changing," he says. "It is the fastest-growing industry in the world. Computers have made communications possible at lightning speed."

Marty cites advances in science, medicine, engineering, law, manufacturing, and education as just some examples of the ways in which computers have changed industry and society. These technological advances are what make his job that much more challenging.

"A typical day for me begins when I arrive at my office about 6:30 A.M.," Marty says. "After running the branch's allocation reports for all the salespeople in our office, I check my voice mail for any emergency issues that must be addressed quickly. An example might be a critical shipment that hasn't arrived on time or a file server that has developed a problem and is inoperable. These situations demand my immediate attention.

"I read my e-mail messages next. It's not unusual to have between five and fifteen messages ranging from company updates to manufacturer price changes to additions and deletions from any number of vendors. Some messages require a response ASAP; others can be addressed during the course of my regular business day.

"Next stop is my in-box, which usually contains a collection of faxes that have arrived since I left the office at the end of business yesterday. These faxes could contain purchase orders, manufac-turer promotional notices, seminar information, or news of a prospective customer looking for a great reseller like ours. All this, and the clock has not yet struck 8 A.M."

Once the official business day begins, Marty handles calls from customers concerning products, services, and orders. A typical day might include a quick staff meeting to discuss changes in plans or a new company procedure. Afternoons are usually spent finishing projects, faxing price quotes, and filing purchase orders and invoices.

In addition to the regular routine, Marty also puts out a special electronic price list every sixty days to reflect constantly changing prices. This process usually takes three to four working days. He also provides a manuscript of more than five thousand items from a third-party vendor. On any given day, he might also accompany a manufacturer to a client facility, where they call on any number of departments that have requested information or a demonstra-tion of a new item.

"My day ends about the time that local traffic starts to build on the highway," Marty says. "This represents a ten-plus-hour day, five days a week, four-point-three weeks a month. To say this is a hectic day is putting it mildly. However, if you enjoy what you do, it can be and is a labor of love.

"The most enjoyable part of my position is helping my customers understand their needs in respect to the use of the equipment," Marty adds. "An example would be a customer interested in a laptop computer to do presentations at remote sites versus a client needing a laptop for communicating to his home base.

"The upside of my business is the satisfaction of being productive and helping others do the same. When I complete a project with confidence in a timely manner so my customers can enjoy productivity, I take a moment to sit back and breathe easy."

Marty also talks about the downside of his career. "If I had to pick a project I least like to perform, it's the tons of paperwork that is a necessary evil in the day-to-day flow of business. The downside is always the fact of being in a race with the clock. I try never to let the clock win. I also refuse to let a discontinued product stop me from saying to customers that I can't fill their needs. Somewhere out there is a replacement part. All salespeople are part detective. We look until we find what we need to help our customers."

Marty offers some advice for anyone thinking about a career in computer sales. "For those who are considering entering my world, I would say to be prepared to plan for a very exciting career. Technology advances as fast as you can absorb yesterday's breakthroughs. Pick a school that offers the career path that you wish to follow (sales and marketing, computer network engineering, or service and repair). Attend as many seminars in the field as possible. Read all the journals that pertain to your area of interest. Spend as much time as you can afford talking to those around you in that particular field. Don't be afraid to roll up your sleeves and get your hands dirty. Ask a million questions. Experiment with the knowledge you've gained. Share your findings with others and always remember that, to achieve success, you must make learning a lifelong endeavor."

Donna Maas, Business Owner and Sales Professional

Donna Maas's formal studies include interior architecture, design, drafting, and oil painting. With a background in graphic art, she designs all marketing materials and packaging for MAAS Polishing Systems of Willowbrook, Illinois. She serves as president and CEO of the company.

After six years of using various cleaning and polishing products and always wishing for something better, Maas asked a chemist to assist her in formulating a product that worked. The end result is MAAS Polishing Creme, a product that quickly restores all metals, fiberglass, Plexiglas and dull, oxidized paintwork to an unusually brilliant finish. "Little did I realize how this innovative formula would revolutionize the polishing products industry," she says.

"The job is glamorous, hectic, and unpredictable," Donna explains. "My role encompasses product development, designing marketing materials, and fielding calls from major retailers while maintaining balance in the offices, warehouse, and factory. This, combined with extensive traveling and television appearances on QVC to demonstrate my products, requires tremendous stamina. Everyone within the company, from my executive assistant to the shipping department, will tell you that every project I tackle must be treated with urgency, requiring immediate attention. This keeps my office personnel (including myself) operating at an unusually fast pace."

Hard work paid off for Donna. By her third year in business, she experienced an 800 percent growth on her initial investment. "It is tremendously fulfilling to obtain such rapid success and world-wide recognition," Donna says. "I would have to think long and hard if asked what the downside of my career is because I can't think of anything!"

Based on her experience, Donna offers some advice for aspiring business owners. "I would advise others who wish to get into this field to stay focused. The most difficult thing for an entrepreneur to do is to focus. You have so many things coming at you all at once. I have learned to concentrate on the most promising opportunities. When you become scattered and attempt to address every opportunity, your success is hindered."

Jim LeClair, Business Owner and Sales Manager

Jim LeClair is the owner and sales manager of Advanced Computer Services in Lawrence, Kansas. He earned a high school diploma and took some secondary accounting and business classes. He also has engaged in ongoing seminars and classes that are offered by suppliers to enhance sales, technical training, and product knowledge.

"I was burned out on retail and on working for others," he says, "so my wife and I decided to form our own business. She had a strong computer background, and I had more of the business background. We felt our strengths would complement one another. Our company consists of training and network installations, network design to integration, support, and fiber optics, to name a few."

Jim's business employs five people who work Monday through Friday from 8 A.M. until 5 P.M. He strives to maintain a relaxed yet professional atmosphere, being mindful of employees' needs and working to keep morale as high as possible.

A typical day in Jim's business is difficult to describe because things can change dramatically on short notice. Jim arrives at work at 7 A.M. and stays until 7 P.M. He spends about 30 percent of his time handling customers' needs, 40 percent working on sales, and 30 percent on the daily activities involved in running the business.

"What I like best," Jim says, "is seeing how happy the customer is when we say, 'This is how the network will work,' and then the network performs as well or better than anticipated. What I like least is having to discipline employees or contemplate lost sales.

"To be successful in this kind of work, it's very important to keep abreast of the current technology at all times, to be a good listener, to be flexible, to be able to read people, and to understand what they *really* want—not what they *say* they want. You have to be able to think quickly on your feet and have a semiaggressive nature. You just can't take no for an answer. Still, you must sell the customers what they want. Don't try to sell people something that isn't right for them just because you can make some money."

Jim's advice to anyone interested in a similar career is based on basic personal traits. "I'd advise those who are considering computer sales to be honest, to be fair, and always to do a good job. Our business has grown because we have gained the trust of both our customers and our employees."

Kathryn M. McKenzie, Sales Representative

Kathryn McKenzie received her bachelor of arts degree in history from Davidson College in Davidson, North Carolina. She is working toward a master's degree in museum studies and textile conservation at the Fashion Institute of Technology in New York. Kathryn is employed as a sales representative for Victor Innovatex/Studio 180, a mill that makes fabric specifically for the office furniture market.

Prior to her current position, Kathryn spent six years working for an office furniture dealer. She began as a project assistant on a project management team working for a bank that was finishing construction of its new headquarters. As the project progressed, Kathryn handled the acquisition of furnishings and coordinated part of the company's move. She ultimately worked as marketing manager for the project and handled proposals, contracts, marketing literature, and events. Kathryn believes that these experiences all served to enhance her skills, and she also learned a lot from her interaction with the sales force.

While she was working for the office furniture dealer, Kathryn decided that she wanted to pursue a career in textiles. She was contacted by a headhunter about a sales position at a textile mill based in Quebec that would allow her to work from home as a sales representative for the Northeast. "My immediate response was 'No way,'" Kathryn says, "because I didn't want a sales position and I didn't have the space to work at home. Then I reconsidered and decided that I should at least go to the interview. Much to my surprise, I got the position and have been enjoying it ever since."

Kathryn considered the position a challenging opportunity to improve her business skills. She had never liked talking with strangers, which she had to do on her very first day on the job. She has also been able to develop strategic thinking skills. Kathryn was also attracted to the position because she felt that her interest in fabric was a good fit in the textile industry, and she wanted to work for a company that made a product.

Kathryn describes her job as a mix of stress and pleasure. "The stress is in meeting numbers and objectives set by me and the sales manager; the pleasure is in being involved in the design process and showing exciting products and capabilities to my customers," she says.

When asked to describe a typical workday, Kathryn says that there really aren't any. Her days generally begin with numerous phone calls, followed by meetings with customers and the design staff. Following customer meetings, Kathryn writes reports for the sales manager and design group detailing what the customers have seen, what they want, and what they expect from the company.

As sales representative, Kathryn acts as liaison, communicator, project manager, and problem solver. She describes her days as generally relaxed, unless a problem arises. She works an average of forty hours a week, but some days are longer than others, especially when she has to travel to meet with customers.

Kathryn finds meeting with customers exciting. "It's definitely enjoyable taking customers out for those necessary business lunches," she says. "However, it's frustrating when you've traveled a distance and no one bothers to show up."

Kathryn sums up how she feels about her job: "What I like most about my work is that I'm involved in textiles and that the clients I deal with are especially nice. I love the challenge of discovering just how my company can fulfill a need for a customer. I enjoy the fact that the days and hours are somewhat flexible—that I set my own schedule. I feel comfortable knowing that the results are based on my efforts and the efforts of the design team. I like building relationships with customers and meeting new people.

"Initially I enjoyed the travel, but as time has gone on, it has become less exciting. I think it has more to do with the familiarity of those places and sometimes the hassles involved in getting to some of the far-flung places I have to go."

Kathryn's advice to others pursuing a career in sales is to accept the challenges it offers. She also recommends being aware of the work environment or corporate culture you are entering. "Sometimes you never know until you get there, but usually there are inklings of what a place will be like. Think about whether you really can work at home and whether you want your boss down the hall or in another country. I never realized what an impact these conditions would have on me.

"But whatever the circumstances, I would say, 'Go for it!' You only live once, and life is not a race. It doesn't matter how you get to the finish line, just so long as you feel you have lived your life completely. If it doesn't work out, chalk it up to experience. If it does work out, then you are all the better for it."

Don Godshaw, Business Owner and Sales Professional

Don Godshaw attended Lakeland College in Plymouth, Wisconsin, where he majored in business administration and economics.

After spending nineteen years in sales, marketing, and product development for the textiles, bag, and sporting goods industries, he is now owner and president of his own company, Travelon, based in Des Plaines, Illinois.

Don was assigned the duties of company president when the former president was dismissed. After running the business for several months, he was surprised when the board chairman promoted him to president. Since that time, Don has purchased the company. Today he is the owner, president, and chairperson of Travelon. Don credits three things with leading to his career path in sporting goods, sales, textiles, and bag manufacturing: early involvement in the sporting goods retail business, a love of skiing, and a talent for sales.

Early in his career, Don worked in a ski shop and learned all aspects of the sport. He advanced from the stock room and service department to sales, display, merchandising, and purchasing. He learned about backpacks, tents, sleeping bags, and other outdoor equipment during this time, fostering his passion for the luggage and travel wear industry.

One of Don's main interests became finding innovative approaches to developing and featuring merchandise. He learned from his own early hiking experience that a better design was needed for the backpack because the weight distribution caused the hiker to look at the ground instead of at the scenery. "This convinced me that there had to be a better way," Don says, "although at that time I never considered that recognizing that problem would become part of my career path."

When he is in the Des Plaines office, Don's day typically begins at 7 A.M. with reading up to twenty pages of overseas e-mail or faxes. He meets with the vice president of sales to receive updates on all of the company's sales activity and handles any issues regarding sales, credit, new product designs, or office politics.

Don keeps an open-door policy and spends a large part of his day fielding staff questions and comments. Product managers are given specific guidelines for handling most aspects of the business, but because many situations require deviation from standard operating procedure, Don stays closely involved with most aspects of the business. "The pace is hectic but exceptionally satisfying," he says, "in good part because I have been lucky enough to surround myself with a team of dynamic executives, mostly female, who are intelligent, trustworthy, and passionate about our business."

The pace is accelerated when Don travels for business, which he does approximately 35 percent of the year. While it might seem glamorous, overseas travel to distant exotic places includes putting up with bad water, uncomfortable hotel rooms, and weeks away from family and friends. A typical workday in Asia starts at 6:30 A.M. with a visit to the factory, where Don spends the entire day supervising new product design, negotiating pricing, solving quality problems, and communicating with clients and the home office. After ten to fourteen hours at a factory, he typically returns to his hotel, contacts his office, and goes to sleep.

Don says that the work atmosphere is very important to him. He tries to maintain a casual business attitude throughout the organization, and, although some established rules are needed, the company generally hires people who are diligent self-starters who do not require constant direction. Closed-door meetings are rare, and communications among all levels of the company are clear. "Our people realize that working together positively accomplishes much more than talking about who is doing what to whom," Don says. "The staff works together like a championship-level sports team. The camaraderie and support are like nothing I've seen in my prior business experiences. I'm tremendously proud of the way our people work selflessly toward a common goal."

The aspect of his job that Don enjoys most is the creative merchandising and marketing—determining a target customer, developing a product strategy, and then presenting that concept with the strength of the organization behind it. He takes great satisfaction in knowing that every department—product design, manufacturing, importation, product management, distribution, and finance—is fully ready, willing, and able to work with other departments to successfully complete every project.

Don describes his least favorite aspect of the business as "dealing with those customers who appear to feel that they are doing us a favor in allowing us to sell to them. I look to our relationships with our customers as strategic partnerships, and a partnership needs to be good for both parties. Once in a while, we deal with clients who feel that only their needs must be satisfied and that our needs are secondary."

Don is certain about the main reason for Travelon's success. He says, "I attribute our success to the highly talented people we've been fortunate enough to be able to assemble. It's relatively simple to build some good products in any field but extremely difficult over the long term to hold together a good organization of people. As a leader, I realize it is my job to try to be considerate of the financial and emotional needs of our staff members. With that accomplished, we can continue to have a winning team."

For More Information

The following professional associations can provide additional information about each category of sales.

Retail Sales

Information on careers in retail sales may be obtained from the personnel offices of local stores, state merchants' associations, or local chapters of the United Food and Commercial Workers union. Visit the website at www.ufcw.org.

In addition, general information about retailing is available from:

National Retail Federation
325 Seventh Street NW, Suite 1100
Washington, DC 20004
www.nrf.com

Services Sales

For details about employment opportunities for services sales representatives, contact employers who sell services in your area.

For information on careers and scholarships in hotel management and sales, contact:

The American Hotel & Lodging Association (AH&LA)
1201 New York Avenue NW, Suite 600
Washington, DC 20005
www.ahla.com

Manufacturing and Wholesale Sales

Information on manufacturers' agents is available from:

Sales and Marketing Executives International
PO Box 1390
Sumas, WA 98295
www.smei.org

Insurance Sales

General occupational information about insurance agents and brokers is available from the home office of many life and casualty insurance companies. Information on state licensing requirements may be obtained from the department of insurance at any state capital.

For information about insurance sales careers in independent agencies and brokerages, contact:

National Association of Professional Insurance Agents
400 North Washington Street
Alexandria, VA 22314
www.pianet.com

For information about professional designation programs, contact:

National Alliance for Insurance Education and Research
3630 North Hills Drive
Austin, TX 78731
www.scic.com

CPCU Society: The Professional Association for Chartered
    Property and Casualty Underwriters
720 Providence Road
Malvern, PA 19355
www.cpcusociety.org

Real Estate Sales

Details on licensing requirements for real estate agents, brokers, and appraisers are available from most local real estate and appraiser organizations or from the state real estate commission or board.

For more information about opportunities in real estate work, contact:

National Association of Realtors
30700 Russell Ranch Road
Westlake Village, CA 91362
www.realtor.com

Information on careers and licensing and certification requirements in real estate appraising is available from:

American Society of Appraisers
555 Herndon Parkway, Suite 125
Herndon, VA 20170
www.appraisers.org

Appraisal Institute
550 West Van Buren Street, Suite 1000
Chicago, IL 60607
www.appraisalinstitute.org

Travel Sales

Information on sales careers in the travel industry can be obtained from:

American Society of Travel Agents
1101 King Street, Suite 200
Alexandria, VA 22314
www.astanet.com

Association of Retail Travel Agents
3161 Custer Drive, Suite 8
Lexington, KY 40517
www.artaonline.com

The Travel Institute (Institute of Certified Travel Agents)
148 Linden Street, Suite 305
Wellesley, MA 02482
www.thetravelinstitute.com

CHAPTER TWO

Careers in Public Relations and Fund-Raising

The most amazing feature of American life is its boundless publicity. Everybody has to meet everybody, and they seem to enjoy this enormity.

—Carl Jung

HELP WANTED: PUBLIC RELATIONS COORDINATOR

Chicago-based firm seeks professional with three years of experience in communications, media relations, or public relations. Strong business-to-business technology or information systems background preferred. We seek someone who is adept at strategic thinking, plan development, and implementation.

Excellent feature and article writing skills with strong knowledge of print communications (newsletters, press releases, magazines, journals), direct mail, image building, conference marketing, and advertising and promotional copywriting are required. Creativity and a fresh approach are essential, as are desktop publishing and production experience. We offer competitive wages and a strong benefits package. Forward your resume with salary history.

....

Public Relations

You might be surprised to learn that the concept of public relations is hardly a new invention. It goes all the way back to 1787, during the time of the Constitutional Convention. And in the 1800s, both the North and the South made use of the media during the Civil War in an attempt to persuade the populace to adopt their way of thinking.

Today, the goal of public relations remains the same—to sway the public in a particular direction or to build, maintain, and promote positive relationships between two factions: the agencies (or companies) and the public.

Public Relations Professionals

Public relations professionals may operate as self-employed consultants or as employees of public relations companies. They may also find work in the PR departments of a variety of entities, such as political parties, nonprofit organizations, hospitals, colleges and universities, trade unions, financial institutions, social service organizations, or clothing companies.

Business and industry rely on corporate public relations to educate the public about products and services. And because many nonprofit organizations do very little advertising, they count on public service announcements created by public relations professionals to get their word out.

Possible Job Settings

The work of a public relations practitioner falls into six main categories:

1. **Research.** This includes all of the preliminary work that is undertaken to determine the client's goals so that a plan to achieve them can be devised. Library and Internet research,

client interviews, surveys, opinion polls, and data collection are all part of this.

2. **Program work.** Once research is completed, a plan is established based upon the findings.

3. **Writing and editing.** This may include press releases, presentations to clients, internal memos, reports, and magazine articles.

4. **Special events.** Included in this category are press conferences, special appearances, and autograph signings. All are carefully orchestrated to gain the greatest amount of attention.

5. **Media placement.** It is important to select the most important information to release, choose the best time to release it, and send it to the most advantageous receivers.

6. **Fund-raising.** Fund-raising is what sustains nonprofit organizations. Possible events include membership drives, direct solicitation, and benefit banquets.

Those who work as generalists in the field must be able to perform a wide array of duties at the same time. In any given week, a public relations professional may write press releases for one client, design a brochure for another, approach an editor for a third, meet with a talk show host for a fourth, implement a promotion for a fifth, set up a press conference for a sixth, put together a press kit for a seventh, work out the beginnings of a client contact for an eighth, and field media questions for a ninth!

In the governmental arena, public relations specialists may be called press secretaries, communications specialists, or information officers. A senator's press secretary informs the elected official's constituents of his or her accomplishments and responds to questions from the media and the press. The press secretary schedules and appears at press conferences and issues statements from his or her superior.

Qualifications and Training

There are no defined standards for entry into a public relations career. A college degree combined with public relations experience, usually gained through an internship, is considered excellent preparation for public relations work; in fact, internships are becoming vital to obtaining employment. The ability to communicate effectively is essential. Many entry-level public relations specialists have a college major in public relations, journalism, advertising, or communication.

Some firms seek college graduates who have worked in electronic or print journalism. Other employers seek applicants with demonstrated communication skills and training or experience in a field related to the firm's business—information technology, health, science, engineering, sales, or finance, for example.

Many colleges and universities offer bachelor's and postsecondary degrees in public relations, usually in a journalism or communications department. In addition, many other colleges offer at least one course in this field. A common public relations sequence includes courses in public relations principles and techniques; public relations management and administration, including organizational development; writing, emphasizing news releases, proposals, annual reports, scripts, speeches, and related items; visual communications, including desktop publishing and computer graphics; and research, emphasizing social science research and survey design and implementation. Courses in advertising, journalism, business administration, finance, political science, psychology, sociology, and creative writing are also helpful. Specialties are offered in public relations for business, government, and nonprofit organizations.

Many colleges help students gain part-time internships in public relations that provide valuable experience and training. The U.S. Armed Forces also provide excellent opportunities to gain training and experience. Membership in local chapters of the Public Relations Student Society of America (affiliated with the Public Relations Society of America) or the International Association of Business Communicators provides an opportunity for students to exchange views with public relations specialists and to make professional contacts that may help them find a job in the field. A portfolio of published articles, television or radio programs, slide presentations, and other work is an asset in finding a job. Writing for a school publication or television or radio station provides valuable experience and material for one's portfolio.

Creativity, initiative, good judgment, and the ability to express thoughts clearly and simply are essential in this field. Decision-making, problem-solving, and research skills also are important. People who choose public relations as a career need an outgoing personality, self-confidence, an understanding of human psychology, and an enthusiasm for motivating people. They should be competitive yet able to function as part of a team and be open to new ideas.

Some organizations, particularly those with large public relations staffs, have formal training programs for new employees. In smaller organizations, new employees work under the guidance of experienced staff members. Beginners often maintain files of material about company activities, scan newspapers and magazines for appropriate articles to clip, and assemble information for speeches and pamphlets. They also may answer calls from the press and public, work on invitation lists and details for press conferences, or escort visitors and clients. After gaining experience, they write news releases, speeches, and articles for publication or design and carry out public relations programs. Public relations specialists in smaller firms usually get all-around experience, whereas those in larger firms tend to be more specialized.

Getting Ahead

Promotion to supervisory jobs may come as public relations specialists show that they can handle more demanding assignments. In public relations firms, a beginner might be hired as a research assistant or account coordinator and be promoted to account executive, senior account executive, account manager, and, eventually, vice president. A similar career path is followed in corporate public relations, although the titles may differ. Some experienced public relations specialists start their own consulting firms.

The Public Relations Society of America accredits public relations specialists who have at least five years of experience in the field and have passed a comprehensive six-hour examination (five hours written, one hour oral).

The International Association of Business Communicators also has an accreditation program for professionals in the communication field, including public relations specialists. Those who meet all the requirements of the program earn the Accredited Business Communicator (ABC) designation. Candidates must have at least five years of experience in a communication field and pass a written and oral examination. They also must submit a portfolio of work samples demonstrating involvement in a range of communication projects and a thorough understanding of communication planning.

Employers may consider professional recognition through accreditation a sign of competence in this field, which could be especially helpful in a competitive job market.

Salaries

Median annual earnings for salaried public relations specialists were $43,830 in 2004. The middle 50 percent earned between $32,970 and $59,360, and the lowest 10 percent earned less than $25,750. The top 10 percent earned more than $81,120. Median annual earnings in the industries employing the largest numbers of public relations specialists were as follows:

Advertising and related services	$50,450
Management of companies and enterprises	$47,330
Business, professional, labor, political, and similar organizations	$45,400
Local government	$44,500
Colleges, universities, and professional schools	$39,610

Words from the Pros

The following professionals have shared their experiences about working in public relations. Read their accounts to see whether this challenging field might be right for you.

Tracy Larrua, Senior Account Executive

Tracy Larrua has more than twenty years of experience in public relations, marketing, and advertising. She attended a performing arts high school then entered business college, but ultimately she went to work at an advertising agency instead of completing her degree.

Tracy quickly worked her way up the ladder in advertising after six years as an account executive with Ogilvie and Mather. She then began working in public relations, where she has stayed ever since.

In her native Hawaii, Tracy was the owner of TL Promotes prior to relocating to Los Angeles in 1992. She is active in the culinary, visual arts, and music arenas, and she currently represents musicians, artists, and a production company.

"My typical day is spent writing pitch letters; developing story ideas for editors; and adding, deleting, and updating our media database to be as up-to-date as possible with what is going on with our clients," says Tracy. "While wearing a headset, I also make a lot of phone calls. The atmosphere is never relaxed. Actually, it is usually very high stress, but it's a *fun* stress. Our typical work week is forty-plus hours, but depending on client demand, workload, and editorial deadlines, it can easily turn into a sixty-plus week."

Tracy has some advice for anyone considering a career in public relations. "I would recommend that others who are interested in entering this profession get in on the ground floor and act like a sponge. Soak up everything you can," she stresses. "As you start developing your skills, you'll find yourself ascending. Also, stay flexible. This industry has gone through all sorts of changes. Learn, adapt, and adopt a fearless attitude."

Tracy also adds a word of caution: "If you aren't the 'people type,' don't even consider getting into this business. You have to be comfortable and persuasive in talking to people—all kinds of people. Remember, your personality skills count for a lot in this industry."

Betsy Nichol, Public Relations Business Owner

Betsy Nichol heads her own public relations agency, Nichol & Company of New York. She earned a bachelor of science degree in journalism from Boston University and has continued to enhance her credentials through seminars and professional workshops.

Like many public relations specialists, Betsy began her career as a journalist. She served a three-month internship at Fairchild Publications and ultimately held a full-time position at its publication *Home Furnishings Daily*. After three years, Betsy was recruited by a small public relations firm.

"Early on in my career," Betsy says, "someone told me I should have my own business, and at the time I thought he was crazy, but as the years went by I realized that I'm one of those people who is better at being my own boss than working for someone else."

Betsy's initial attraction to the field of public relations was its fast pace and varied responsibilities. She was interested in meeting people from different professions and having the opportunity to learn about many different subjects.

"I also like to communicate in writing," says Betsy, "and good writing skills are essential in the PR business. There's never a dull moment in this business, and being successful requires many of the same skills as being a journalist. It's been an exciting journey.

"Being head of a public relations firm is very hectic," Nichol stresses. "The phone is always ringing, and you never know if it's a client with a crisis, an editor on a deadline, or an employee with a question."

As head of the agency, Betsy spends a good deal of time in meetings with clients or consulting with them by telephone. She also meets with employees to discuss their progress on various projects. In addition, she attends to new business, keeps up with industry standards, and monitors her company accordingly. To accomplish all of this, Betsy continually monitors her e-mail; talks on the phone; gives instructions to staff; and addresses faxes, notes, and mail that require her attention.

Networking is also an important part of Betsy's career. She attends and speaks at many meetings, workshops, and other events that can lead to new business, provide insight into industry trends, and form alliances that enable her to better serve her clients.

Betsy talks about the ups and downs of her profession. "The public relations business offers endless ways to express one's creativity. It also demands that one think strategically to help clients solve their problems, which keeps me on my toes and makes every day action packed.

"In running a business of twelve people, there is also a great sense of teamwork and caring among the staffers—not a typical office environment. The interaction between us produces exciting results and great fun. The downside is that we often have to cancel evening plans and work late to meet breaking deadlines."

Betsy Nichol offers a suggestion to those interested in public relations. "My advice to others who are considering this field is to work hard and be flexible and both patient and impatient in your quest for success."

Karen Bierman, Publicist

Karen Bierman received a bachelor of arts degree from Cornell University in Ithaca, New York. She works as a publicist at Planned Television Arts in New York.

Karen's career in the film industry began right after college, when a friend recommended that she apply for an internship at Columbia/TriStar. As a movie buff with an interest in public relations, she decided to apply and was accepted for the intern position. Karen feels that she learned a lot about the industry during this time because there were relatively few interns and the people she worked with were willing to share their knowledge.

After her internship, Karen worked with a film company, hoping to advance her knowledge of the industry. However, because the PR departments of New York film companies are relatively small, full-time jobs are difficult to find. She decided to try working in the theater instead and was hired for a research position by Actors' Equity. Although Karen loved the company, her real interest was in public relations. After applying again to all of the film companies and publicity agencies in New York, she was offered a position at Baker Winokur Ryder Public Relations. During her two and a half years there, Karen worked as office assistant, assistant publicist to the vice president of publicity/director of the New York office, and junior publicist.

Karen describes the main focus of public relations as getting to know the client or project to which you are assigned and the media you will be working with. What this means in reality is making hundreds of phone calls each day, scheduling photo shoots, screenings, interviews, and personal appearances; securing invitations to events; getting clothing for the client to wear; and arranging travel and transportation. Some projects involve a lot of writing, and there are often many faxes to send as well as the press materials to mail. Many publicists write their clients' bios and pitch letters.

In addition, publicists may be called upon to chaperone clients, which involves accompanying them at interviews and appearances and making sure that everything goes smoothly.

Karen says that the atmosphere in PR work can range from stressful to relaxed, depending on the project. The work is most demanding when a deadline is looming or she is working on a high-profile account. During the summer television hiatus, however, things are generally quieter. Overall, the job involves long hours, including many nights and weekends because the events that clients attend are held after normal work hours and press junkets are often held on weekends. Publicists must often escort a client to an early morning television interview and then attend a film premier late the same evening.

When asked to offer advice for others interested in public relations work, Karen says, "I would stress that patience is truly a virtue in this business. It can be really difficult to get your foot in the door, so try to get internships over the summer and during the school year. Most schools give you credit for these internships. And networking is also very important. If you meet people through internships or at parties, keep in touch with them. You never know who might be the one to help provide your big break. Also, many companies like to promote from within, so if you are offered a job that you think is beneath you, it might still be worthwhile to take it and prove to them that you are worthy of a promotion. It really helps to be an outgoing, vivacious person, as you really need to not only 'sell' your client but yourself as well. Remember that appearance is also important—you always want to dress as if you've already received that next promotion."

Joanne Levine, Public Relations Professional and Business Owner

Joanne Levine owns Chicago-based Lekas & Levine Public Relations, which specializes in pursuing media publicity for small and mid-sized businesses.

Joanne did not enter the field in the usual way. She majored in English in college and had no ambition to focus on public relations. She joined local community groups while raising her children, and this became a stepping-stone to her future career. While setting up a fund-raiser for one of the organizations, Joanne worked with a public relations professional on the publicity committee. She learned a lot from the experience and became fascinated by the work.

During this time, Joanne's brother was creating and marketing original adult board games. To test her skills, Joanne wrote and sent out a press release each time he introduced a new game. One game even included Joanne as a character. When the local press picked up the story, she and her brother got both local and national coverage.

"That first project really whet my appetite," Joanne says. "From there, I began publicizing my husband's retail stores, more civic groups, and the like. One day, I thought about the fact that I was doing a great job and not getting paid for it. I recruited my brother's wife to help me, and we wrote a press release about two sisters-in-law who started a public relations company devoted to small businesses. We got an immediate response from the local chain of newspapers. They wrote a feature article about our company, even though we had no clients. The rest, they say, is history. From that initial article, the phone began to ring, and within a month or two, we had five clients. It's been word of mouth ever since."

Joanne describes media public relations as popular among clients but stressful for the PR professional. In addition to writing copy for brochures and planning special events, Joanne estimates that 80 percent of her time is spent helping her clients to appear in newspapers, magazines, and trade publications, as well as on television and radio. Media publicity increases a client's visibility and adds credibility to a client's reputation.

Despite the appeal of media publicity to clients, it is not as popular among the public relations professionals who must do the work. As Joanne says, "With an ad, you know what day it will appear, what size it will be, and exactly what it will say. With an article, I hold my breath until the client and I read it in the publication. With a taped interview on radio or television, I wait to see if anything was cut or taken out of context. While my press release and phone conversation with an editor might have been chock-full of the kind of information I hope they will relay to the public, there are no guarantees such as those in advertising. I work with editors and writers who are always on deadline, always overworked, but nevertheless always looking for a good angle. For these reasons, my job can be stressful and sometimes plagued with problems that are completely out of my control."

Despite the pressure, Joanne finds that the positive aspects of her work outweigh the negative. "When all goes well, there's nothing like it," she says. "I have seen the positive results of good, steady media campaigns time and time again. And more than once in a while, a really big media appearance can make an overnight difference in someone's business. The client is on cloud nine, his or her phones begin to ring off the hook with new business, and I am showered with praise and gratitude. I often get to know my clients well and enjoy friendly, upbeat working relationships with them. The knowledge that I am helping to make a client's business grow is very rewarding."

Based on her experience, Joanne offers some practical advice for aspiring public relations specialists: "If you want a career in media publicity, I would advise you to read, read, read. Study the format of newspapers, watch the twelve, five, six, and ten o'clock news. Read every magazine you can get your hands on and note how things are laid out. Reporters have certain 'beats,' and if you can zero in on what they write about, half the battle is won. Familiarizing oneself with the media is a never-ending responsibility. While there are a few good media guides that provide information, this is not a substitute for studying the style of an individual person, section, or publication. Also, as the media faces the same cutbacks and consolidations as any other industry, frequent changes in personnel happen at a rapid pace."

For those seeking a more traditional route, Joanne suggests looking for an internship with a PR company. Also, she has personally used graduate students as freelancers several times.

Joanne stresses that a successful PR person must be original. "Just remember that in order to make it in this field, you need a good imagination and the ability to find an 'angle,'" she says. "I can't tell you how many times a client has said, 'I do a better job than anyone else in town, and I truly care about my customers.'

That's very nice, but it's boring! Find out why the client does a better job. What does he or she do differently? Is the business owner an interesting person? What are his or her hobbies? The list goes on and on. You must be able to pick someone's brain until something newsworthy pops out. Then, you must learn who might be fascinated with your information, so much so that they want to inform their readers about it or share it with their television audience."

····························

Fund-Raising

> **HELP WANTED: DIRECTOR OF RESOURCE DEVELOPMENT**
> Seeking an experienced fund-raising professional with a demonstrated success with private and corporate foundations and development of major donors; exceptional oral and written communication; solid research, planning, and grant-writing skills; strong skills in developing relationships; solid business, goal-driven, and results orientation; dynamic personality; initiative; and a creative approach to resource development. Submit resume, related writing sample, and salary requirements.

As this want ad illustrates, fund-raisers need a broad range of skills to be involved in planning and organizing programs designed to raise money. They work for educational, historical, community, religious, arts, cultural, educational, social service, health, advocacy, political, trade, scientific, and research organizations. They may also promote youth leadership and other charitable causes. Sometimes referred to as philanthropy, the fund-raising industry ranks as one of the ten largest in the United States.

Fund-raisers are usually asked to determine the length and scope of the campaign, develop slogans or other phrases associated with the effort, decide how funds will be solicited, and assign responsibility for who will carry out these tasks. Then they oversee the efforts to make sure things stay on schedule and go according to plan. They regularly assess and reassess the campaign to determine what changes may be needed.

With enthusiasm, energy, and competence, fund-raisers combine the skills of financial management, public relations, marketing, accounting, human resources, personnel management, and media communications. Assessing the viability of charitable programs, they devise strategies for meeting goals, identify potential donors, and solicit funds efficiently and effectively. In the 1990s alone, Americans contributed more than $100 trillion to educational, health, research, arts, religious, and social welfare organizations.

Fund-raisers may be known as any of the following:

- Director of Major Donor Development
- Director of Annual Giving
- Director of Major Gifts
- Development Director
- Director of Development
- Vice President for Development
- Sponsorship Director
- Director of Resource Development
- Fund-Raising CEO
- Fund-Raising Coordinator
- Fund-Raising Researcher
- Membership Director
- Development Research Coordinator

Job Settings for Fund-Raisers

Fund-raisers fall into one of three general categories. The first group consists of staff members of health centers, social services agencies, community groups, nonprofit organizations, and cultural institutions. In each case, they plan and work on all fundraising projects. For instance, a fund-raiser who is employed by a college may write to large corporations to solicit contributions.

The second group of fund-raisers works for fund-raising consulting firms. These individuals provide advice to nonprofit organizations about the best ways to raise money and manage the funds they accumulate. For instance, a hospital that is interested in raising money might hire the services of a fund-raising consultant.

The third group of fund-raisers works for companies that specialize in offering fund-raising events for any organization that wishes to raise money. This, for instance, might include carnivals, concerts, and theater parties.

Fund-raisers often work in temporary locations. They attend meetings, present talks, and meet with volunteers. As the campaign progresses, tension grows and the pace becomes increasingly hectic. With the stress of meeting financial goals within a limited time period, fund-raisers often need to work long hours—perhaps seven-day weeks—in order to meet the designated goals.

Qualifications and Training

Most fund-raisers have liberal arts degrees, though the degree specialty varies, and different organizations may require specific qualifications. If you know in advance that you wish to do fundraising for an environmental concern, for example, then it would be best to focus on a degree in something related, such as environmental studies.

Marketing degrees are also helpful, as is practical knowledge from courses such as mathematics, economics, computers, bookkeeping, and accounting. Other suggested courses include psychology, speech, sociology, public relations, social work, education, journalism, and business administration.

Individuals considering this line of work should have strong communication and numerical skills and be well organized and flexible. They must also be able to work well with others, to work under pressure, and to meet deadlines.

Fund-raisers must be capable writers and motivators. Sales skills are a requirement, as are computer skills. Fund-raisers may use special software, such as donor tracking programs, in their work.

Most employers seek individuals with two to seven years of experience. Internships and volunteer opportunities are ways to get experience, and nonprofits have many more volunteer opportunities than do business or government agencies. With five years of experience—paid or unpaid—you may choose to become certified by the Association of Fundraising Professionals.

Salaries

Fund-raisers can work as unpaid volunteers or earn as much as $200,000 per year. The median annual salary for fund-raisers is $52,000, but the range of compensation is extreme, depending on a variety of factors: the size of the organization, whether it is nonprofit or for profit, years of experience, and geographical location. Here are some average yearly salaries:

Entry-level fund-raising director	$35,000
Program manager	$48,000
Senior-level director	$51,833
Consultant	$75,000

Qualified fund-raisers are in high demand. Because the federal government has cut back on spending in the areas of cultural and social programs, the burden of charitable activity has been thrust upon philanthropic sources.

Words from a Pro

Following is a personal account of someone who works in fund-raising. Read on to learn firsthand what the career is really like.

Thomas Campbell, Director of Development and Alumni Relations

Thomas L. Campbell earned his bachelor of science degree in business administration in 1981 and a master of science degree in physical education in 1987 from the University of Delaware. He also received a master's in business administration from Wilkes University in 1990. He is a Certified Fundraising Executive (Association of Fundraising Professionals) and serves as director of development and alumni relations at Allentown College of St. Francis de Sales in Center Valley, Pennsylvania.

Thomas's career at Allentown began almost by accident. In 1988 he was interested in relocating to Pennsylvania from Florida, and he considered his interview at Allentown College as good practice for beginning his job search. He was offered the job, which he decided to accept and keep for a few years before moving on. Thomas has stayed with the job since that time because he loves it.

"Because I had always worked in sales, the work involved was really not that dissimilar," Thomas says. "I found that fund-raising was just another version of sales but with a wonderful twist. The work was now impacting students' lives. I know that without the money I raise, many of our students just wouldn't be able to attend college. And because I recognize the value of a college education and the impact it can have on someone's life, I am very motivated to do this kind of work."

Because fund-raising can be a complex job, Thomas says that his workdays are usually different. There are no typical days, because so many factors go into raising money. A successful fund-raiser must be able to identify potential donors, build relationships, and cultivate them in order to establish a positive encounter.

For Thomas, the job has more positive than negative aspects. "This kind of work brings much joy and is very fulfilling," he says.

"I would say that the most difficult aspect of this position is that it is sometimes difficult to rise to the challenge of exceeding the previous year's performance."

Thomas offers some advice for anyone considering a career in fund-raising: "I would advise others who are interested in entering this career to first secure another type of job on the corporate side. With that kind of experience to your credit, you are a much stronger fund-raiser because you understand what executives must deal with and what they are up against."

For More Information

The following professional associations can aid in your job search. Many of the publications these organizations produce are available in public libraries.

Members of the National Council for Marketing and Public Relations are communications specialists working within community colleges in areas including alumni, community, government, media, and public relations as well as marketing, publications, and special events. The association works to foster improved relations between two-year colleges and their communities. The association holds an annual conference with exhibits, national surveys, and needs assessments. The association also publishes newsletter called "Counsel," which provides information about career opportunities as well as changes in the public relations industry. Additional information about the association can be obtained by contacting:

National Council for Marketing and Public Relations
PO Box 336039
Greeley, CO 80633
www.ncmpr.org

For additional information about careers in public relations, contact the following organizations:

Canadian Public Relations Society
Career File
PO Box 24, Station B
Toronto, ON M5T 2T2
Canada
www.pub-rels.com

Institute for Public Relations
PO Box 118400
2096 Weimer Hall
Gainesville, FL 32611

International Association of Business Communicators
One Hallidie Plaza, Suite 600
San Francisco, CA 94102
www.iabc.com

Public Relations Society of America
33 Maiden Lane, Eleventh Floor
New York, NY 10038
www.prsa.org

Public Relations Student Society of America
33 Maiden Lane, Eleventh Floor
New York, NY 10038
www.prssa.org

Information about careers in fund-raising can be obtained by contacting:

Association of Fundraising Professionals
1101 King Street, Suite 700
Alexandria, VA 22314
www.afpnet.org

Association for Healthcare Philanthropy
313 Park Avenue, Suite 400
Falls Church, VA 22046
www.ahp.org

Direct Marketing Fundraisers Association
224 Seventh Street
Garden City, NY 11530
www.dmfa.org

CHAPTER THREE

Careers in Marketing and Advertising

Promise, large promise, is the soul of an advertisement.
—Samuel Johnson

HELP WANTED: BRAND MARKETING MANAGERS

A leading New York–based confectionery company is seeking results-oriented, creative thinkers to be responsible for fueling profitable growth. You will lead strategic and tactical execution for retail, mail order, and market sales channels; develop strategies, objectives, and tactics to maximize retail profit and loss performance; and execute annual marketing plan. Conducting and analyzing consumer research, you will execute all aspects of developing new products, develop new merchandising approaches to maximize product shelf impact, and lead consumer communication, including advertising, consumer promotions, and public relations.

Qualified candidates must possess three or more years of experience in a consumer packaged goods/retail environment with experience in hands-on product development and construction of annual marketing, product, and store merchandising plans. College degree required; M.B.A. preferred. Interested parties please send resume and salary history.

D oes the previous ad sound interesting to you? Do you enjoy the prospect of helping companies to determine what the needs and desires of the public really are? If so, you might want to consider a career in marketing or advertising!

Marketing Professionals

There is no mistaking the goal of marketing, regardless of the organization or situation. It is to motivate or persuade people to take a specific action: to buy a product or service; to adopt an idea or cause; to provide political support; or to change an opinion.

Firms need to market their products or services profitably. To do so, an overall marketing policy must be established, including product development, market research, market strategies, sales approaches, advertising outlets, promotion possibilities, and effective pricing and packaging.

The Role of the Marketer

Simply stated, marketers try to figure out what consumers have a need for, and salespeople try to encourage people to buy what they are selling. Marketers start at the beginning of the cycle by looking at potential customers and asking, "What do they need?" Once that is determined, marketers look at their companies and ask, "Do we know how to produce it, and can we make money doing it?"

Marketing executives determine the demand for products and services offered by the firm and identify potential consumers, including business firms, wholesalers, retailers, government, or the general public. Mass markets are further categorized according to various factors such as region, age, income, and lifestyle.

In small firms, all marketing responsibilities may be assumed by the owner or chief executive officer. In large firms, which may offer numerous products and services nationally or even globally, experienced professionals work together to coordinate these and related activities.

Once marketers come up with product ideas that may have originated from talking to customers or been generated during brainstorming sessions, they begin communicating with product development departments. In some industries, these might be scientists or engineers. A team forms that includes marketing management, marketing researchers, engineers, advertisers, financial advisors, and, eventually, salespeople.

First the team engages in market research, which determines if the product idea is something the customers really want. Market researchers set up focus groups, bringing groups of consumers together to discuss what isn't working in their present environments and what they truly need.

Professionals working in market research departments are tuned in to the consumer—what he or she worries about, desires, thinks, believes, and holds dear. Market researchers conduct surveys or one-on-one interviews, utilize existing research, test consumer reactions to new products or advertising copy, track sales figures and buying trends, and become overall experts on consumer behavior. Marketing research assistants report directly to a research executive and are responsible for compiling and interpreting data and monitoring the progress of research projects.

Agency research departments design questionnaires or other methods of studying groups of people, implement the surveys, and interpret the results. Sometimes research departments hire an outside market research firm to take over some of the workload. For example, a market researcher could come up with a procedure to test the public's reaction to a television commercial; the outside firm would put the procedure into action.

After the market research is conducted, marketers attempt to quantify a need for the product in the marketplace. For example, if thirty people have said they need a particular device, this suggests a strong need. However, the company can't afford to build something for just thirty people and must make sure that enough people are willing to buy the product. This sparks another round of research. Marketing experts need to know how fast the product can be made, how quickly it can be offered to the public, how many will be bought, and how large the profit will be.

Based on successful research results, marketers begin the concept development stage. This is the development of a word or paragraph that describes the product. In some cases, marketers present this to engineers, who develop a prototype. The prototype is taken to the marketplace for testing and evaluations. With feedback in hand, the team begins to make product improvements.

Once the company is at least 95 percent sure this is the product people want, it's given a final test in the marketplace. The marketing team also tests for claims. For example, a company might want to claim that its new hospital bed will prevent skin sores, but it needs to be able to document that claim.

If all test results point to being able to move forward, the engineers start figuring out how to mass produce the product and marketers plan how the company can make money on it. For that, they have to look at the production cost and determine how much customers would be willing to pay for it. One misconception is that a profit percentage is simply added to the production cost, resulting in the selling price. In reality, prices are not determined that way; they are determined on the basis of what people are willing to pay.

The next step is promotion planning. Now that the company has a product, it has to find a way to get the word out. The appropriate team members make brochures and design advertising. At the same time, other team members are crunching numbers and setting up production schedules.

Once a date is set for introducing the product, the sales force is brought in and taught how to present it. Then the product is monitored to see if it is meeting its sale projections. If it is not, management wants to know why and what is going to be done about it. In fact, even if it is meeting or exceeding expectations, management still wants to know why. That's the way it goes in a competitive business.

Job Settings for Marketing Professionals

Marketing professionals are found in virtually every industry, including motor vehicles, printing and publishing, retail, computer and data processing services, management and public relations, and advertising.

Because marketers and advertising professionals work hand in hand, many marketing departments are located within corporate advertising departments or within private advertising agencies. Private marketing firms function similarly to advertising agencies and work toward the same goals—identifying and targeting specific audiences that will be receptive to specific products, services, or ideas.

Experts advise beginning your job search before you near graduation. Those who arrange internships have an edge; they've already become familiar faces on the job. When an opening comes up, a known commodity—someone who performed well during the internship—is likely to be chosen over an unknown one.

Learn as much as you can about the agency or firm you're interested in. In other words, target your prospects.

The Downsides

Although marketing is considered by many to be a step up from sales, it does have a few downsides. If a company is not making the expected profit, marketers can easily lose their jobs. Their responsibilities for sales volume and profit are the same as those that salespeople must meet.

In essence, marketers make an agreement with sales departments and personnel. For example, they may think, "OK, we are going to sell a hundred units of product X to a particular customer." But if too much money is spent in product development or advertising and only ninety units are sold, although the sales-person has the first responsibility, the marketing team is also responsible. They had agreed on what could be sold on the basis of specific advertising and on setting a certain price. If the mark is missed, the marketers' jobs are also on the line.

Another downside is that marketers usually supervise sales-people, but the sales force often makes more money than the marketers do—sometimes a *lot* more money. But to make up for it, marketers usually also receive a good pension plan and bonuses.

Marketers work long hours, often including evenings and week-ends. Working under pressure is unavoidable as schedules change, problems arise, and deadlines and goals must be met.

Qualifications and Training

A wide range of educational backgrounds is suitable for entry into marketing jobs, but many employers prefer those with experience in related occupations plus a broad liberal arts background. A bachelor's degree in sociology, psychology, literature, journalism, or philosophy, among other subjects, is acceptable. However, requirements vary, depending upon the particular job.

Some employers prefer a bachelor's or master's degree in busi-ness administration with an emphasis in marketing. Courses in business law, economics, accounting, finance, mathematics, and statistics are advantageous. In highly technical industries, such as computer and electronics manufacturing, a bachelor's degree in engineering or science, combined with a master's degree in busi-ness administration, is preferred.

Courses in management and completion of an internship while in school are highly recommended. Familiarity with word pro-cessing and database applications is also important for many posi-tions. Computer skills are vital because marketing, product promotion, and advertising on the Internet are increasingly common. The ability to communicate in a foreign language may open up employment opportunities in many rapidly growing areas around the country, especially in cities with large Spanish-speaking populations.

Those interested in becoming marketing managers should be mature, creative, highly motivated, resistant to stress, flexible, and decisive. The ability to communicate persuasively, both orally and in writing, with other managers, staff, and the public is vital. These managers also need tact, good judgment, and exceptional ability to establish and maintain effective personal relationships with supervisory and professional staff members and client firms.

Getting Ahead

Because of the importance and high visibility of their jobs, marketing managers often are prime candidates for advancement to the highest ranks. Well-trained, experienced, successful managers may be promoted to higher positions in their own, or other, firms. Some become top executives. Managers with extensive experience and sufficient capital even open their own businesses.

Most marketing management positions are filled by promoting experienced staff or related professional personnel. For example, many managers are former sales representatives; purchasing agents; buyers; or product, advertising, promotions, or public relations specialists. In small firms with a limited number of positions, advancement to a management position usually comes slowly. Promotion may occur more quickly in larger firms.

Although experience, ability, and leadership are emphasized for promotion, advancement can be accelerated by participation in management training programs conducted by many large firms. Many firms also provide their employees with continuing education opportunities, either in-house or at local colleges and universities, and encourage employee participation in seminars and conferences, often provided by professional societies.

Several marketing and related associations sponsor national or local management training programs in collaboration with colleges and universities. Course subjects include brand and product management, international marketing, sales management evaluation, telemarketing and direct sales, interactive marketing, promotion, marketing communication, market research, organizational communication, and data processing systems procedures and management. Many firms pay all or part of the cost for those who successfully complete courses.

Some associations offer certification programs for these managers. As a sign of competence and achievement in the field of marketing, certification is particularly important in a competitive job market. For example, Sales and Marketing Executives International offers a management certification program based on education and job performance.

Salaries

According to a survey by the National Association of Colleges and Employers, starting salaries for marketing majors graduating in 2005 averaged $33,873.

Salary levels vary substantially, depending on the level of managerial responsibility, length of service, education, size of firm, location, and industry. For example, manufacturing firms usually pay these managers higher salaries than do nonmanufacturing firms. For sales managers, the size of their sales territory is another important determinant of salary. Many managers earn bonuses equal to 10 percent or more of their salaries.

Median annual earnings for marketing managers were $87,640 in 2004. In the areas employing the largest numbers of marketing managers, average salaries in 2004 were as follows:

Computer systems design and related services	$107,030
Management of companies and enterprises	$98,700
Insurance carriers	$86,810
Architectural, engineering, and related services	$83,610
Depository credit intermediation	$76,450

Advertising

"Priceless." "Don't leave home without it." "The fewest dropped calls." Such phrases are familiar to most of us because of the effective work of advertising specialists. Some consider this phenomenon a nuisance that interrupts television programming and encourages people to buy products that they may not really need. Others look upon it as a great public service. A dominating force in our society, mass-media advertising is a multimillion-dollar industry dating back to the invention of movable type in the mid-1400s.

Job Settings

Virtually every type of business makes use of advertising in some form, often through the services of an advertising agency. Companies look to advertising as a way of boosting sales by increasing the public's awareness of a product.

Most companies do not have staff with the necessary skills or experience to create effective advertisements. In addition, many advertising campaigns are temporary, so employers would have difficulty maintaining their own advertising departments. Instead, companies commonly solicit bids from ad agencies to develop advertising for them. The ad agencies offering their services to the company make presentations to potential clients. The real work for ad agencies begins when they win an account. Various departments within an agency, such as creative, production, media, and research, work together to meet the client's goal of increasing sales.

There are more than fifty thousand advertising and public relations establishments in the United States. About four out of ten write copy and prepare artwork, graphics, and other creative work and then place the resulting ads on television, radio, or the Internet or in periodicals, newspapers, or other media. Within the industry, only these full-service establishments are known as advertising agencies. Many of the largest agencies are international, with a substantial proportion of their revenue coming from abroad.

Most advertising firms specialize in a particular market niche. Some companies produce and solicit outdoor advertising, such as billboards and electric displays. Others place ads in buses, subways, taxis, airports, and bus terminals. A small number of firms produce aerial advertising, while others distribute circulars, handbills, and free samples.

Groups within agencies have been created to serve their clients' electronic advertising needs on the Internet. Online advertisements link users from one website to a company's or product's website, where information such as new product announcements, contests, and product catalogs appears and from which purchases may be made.

Some firms are not involved in the creation of ads at all; instead, they sell advertising time or space on radio and television stations or in publications. Because these firms do not produce advertising, their staffs are mostly sales workers.

The work at an advertising agency is frequently divided among several individuals or departments, usually including:

- **Account executives** make sure that work is completed on time and to the client's satisfaction. Account executives must be savvy about their agencies and aware of each client's desires and needs. Their responsibilities lie more in the business arena than in the creative aspects of advertising.
- **Art directors** must be able to effectively present a theme or idea in convincing visual form through illustration, color, photography, or cinematography.
- **Creative directors** supervise all employees and oversee all activities in the agency. At the top of the hierarchy, creative directors must, of course, be creative as well as possess people skills and solid business acumen.

- **Researchers** seek to determine what kind of audience would be interested in a particular product or service, why they are interested in the product, what messages are most persuasive with each audience, and how the public is reacting to advertising campaigns already in place.
- **Media people** work in the department that ensures that commercials are aired on radio and television and that ads get on the Internet and into magazines and newspapers as planned.

Other advertising positions include television producers, print production managers, graphic artists, illustrators, photographers, freelance writers, print production workers, and traffic managers.

Advertising Copywriters

Advertising copywriters are the real creative force behind ad campaigns. They are the ones who dream up the persuasive words for commercials and advertisements and conjure up the themes for advertising campaigns. Copywriters may also be responsible for creating articles about products or services, sales promotions, public relations materials, billboards, and promotional brochures.

Copywriters usually begin their work by meeting with the client and/or account executive. After gathering as much information as possible, they let their imaginations flow while looking for an idea about why a product or service is different from all others of its kind. Then they proceed to develop a new advertising campaign with their innovative ideas.

Advertising Sales Agents

Advertising sales agents, also called account executives or advertising sales representatives, sell or solicit advertising, including graphic art, advertising space in publications, custom-made signs, or television and radio advertising time. More than half of all advertising sales agents work in the information sector, mostly for media firms, including television and radio broadcasters, print and Internet publishers, and cable program distributors. Other agents work for firms engaged in direct mail advertising or display and outdoor advertising, such as billboards and signs. Because most revenue for magazines, newspapers, directories, and broadcasters is generated from advertising, advertising sales agents play an important role in their success.

Outside sales agents call on clients and prospects at the client's place of business. They may have an appointment, or they may practice cold calling—arriving without an appointment. Inside sales agents work on their employer's premises and handle sales to customers who walk in or telephone the firm to inquire about advertising. Some also may make telephone sales calls—calling prospects, attempting to sell the media firm's advertising space or time, and arranging follow-up appointments between interested prospects and outside sales agents.

Within the advertising industry, media representative firms sell advertising space or time for media owners, including print and Internet publishers, radio and television stations, and cable systems. These firms maintain offices in major cities and employ their own teams of advertising sales agents. The agents they employ work exclusively with the executives at advertising agencies, called media buyers, who purchase advertising space for their clients. Media representative firms may represent any number of publications and radio or television stations, selling space to advertising agencies with clients who want to initiate a national advertising campaign or place advertisements outside their local markets.

Sales agents are employed by local publications or radio and television stations and are responsible for sales in a local territory. Obtaining new accounts is an important part of the job for these agents, who may spend much of their time traveling to visit prospective advertisers and current clients. During a sales call, they discuss the client's advertising needs and suggest how their products and services can meet those needs.

During the first meeting with a client, sales agents gather background information and explain how specific types of advertising will help promote a client's products or services most effectively. Next, the advertising sales agent prepares an advertising proposal to present to the client. This entails determining the advertising medium to be used, preparing sample advertisements, and providing the client with estimates of the cost of the proposal. Consolidation in the media industries has brought the sale of different types of advertising under one roof. Sales are increasingly made of integrated packages that include advertisements to be placed in print, online, and with a broadcast subsidiary.

After a contract has been established, the advertising sales agent serves as the main contact between the client and the firm. The agent handles communication between the parties and assists the client in developing sample artwork or radio and television spots. He or she also arranges for commercial taping sessions and may accompany clients to the sessions.

Beyond selling, advertising sales agents have other duties as well. They analyze sales statistics, prepare reports, and handle the scheduling of their appointments. They read about new and existing products and monitor the sales, prices, and products of their competitors.

In many firms, advertising sales agents handle the drafting of contracts specifying the advertising work to be performed and its cost, as well as the billing and recordkeeping for their customers' accounts, which may include customer service responsibilities such as answering questions or addressing any problems the clients may have with the proposals. Sales agents also are responsible for developing sales tools, promotional plans, and media kits that they use to help make sales.

Qualifications and Training

Most employers expect applicants to have college degrees. For those who aspire to become account executives, an M.B.A. is especially important. Many schools offer programs in advertising, and a number of top advertising agencies offer in-house training programs for copywriters and account managers.

Because copywriters deal with a wide cross section of ideas and concepts, a general liberal arts background in combination with business is particularly valued. Courses in such subjects as economics, history, journalism, marketing, advertising, math, social sciences, speech, literature, business administration, human relations, and creative writing are recommended.

Copywriters need the skills that all writers should have—the ability to produce clear, concise prose. Therefore, writing experience in the form of published articles; participation in school, church, or yearbook publications; work for local newspapers or radio or television studios; and internships are all worthwhile endeavors.

Candidates should prepare a portfolio containing three ads from two or three previous advertising campaigns. These can be class assignments or real ads from actual clients. If you have no advertising experience at all, present potential employers with samples of your published writing.

For advertising sales agents, some employers prefer applicants with a college degree, particularly for sales positions that require meeting with clients. Courses in marketing, leadership, communication, business, and advertising are helpful. For those who sell over the telephone or who have a proven record of successfully selling other products, a high school diploma may be sufficient. After gaining entry into the occupation, successful sales experience becomes more important than education when looking for a position. In general, smaller companies are more willing to hire unproven individuals.

Because they represent their employers to the executives of client organizations, advertising sales agents must have excellent interpersonal and written communication skills. Employers look for applicants who possess a pleasant personality, honesty, and a neat professional appearance. Self-motivation, organization, persistence, independence, and the ability to multitask are required because advertising sales agents set their own schedules and perform their duties without much supervision.

Training takes place mainly on the job. In most cases, an experienced sales manager instructs a newly hired advertising sales agent who lacks sales experience. Advancement means taking on bigger, more important clients. Agents with proven leadership ability and a strong sales record may advance to supervisory and managerial positions such as sales supervisor, sales manager, or vice president of sales. Frequent contact with managers of other departments and people in other firms provides sales agents with leads about job openings, enhancing advancement opportunities.

Salaries

There is a considerable range of salaries in this field, particularly in different regions of the country. The median annual salary in advertising agencies is about $33,000. Junior copywriters may start out in the low twenties; writers with senior status may earn $60,000 to $100,000 and even more as creative directors. Median annual earnings were $63,610 for advertising and promotions managers in 2004.

Most advertising sales workers are paid a combination of salaries, commissions, and bonuses. Commissions are usually based on the amount of sales, whereas bonuses may depend on individual performance, on the performance of all sales workers in the group or district, or on the company's performance. Median annual earnings in 2004 for all advertising sales agents were $40,300, including commissions. The industries hiring the largest numbers of agents are advertising and related services; radio and television broadcasting; and newspaper, periodical, book, and directory publishers.

In addition to their earnings, advertising sales agents usually are reimbursed for expenses such as transportation costs, meals, hotels, and entertaining customers. They often receive benefits such as health and life insurance, pension plans, vacation and sick leave, personal use of a company car, and frequent flier mileage. Some companies offer incentives such as free vacation trips or gifts for outstanding sales workers.

The larger the agency or account, the higher the salary will be. The best locations for jobs are in large cities such as New York, Chicago, Detroit, Boston, Atlanta, Dallas, Minneapolis, San Francisco, and Los Angeles.

Words from the Pros

Read the following personal accounts of advertising professionals to see whether this career might suit your persuasive personality.

Edward Pitkoff, Marketing and Advertising Professional

Edward Pitkoff of Omaha, Nebraska, attended the Philadelphia Museum School of Art, the Pennsylvania Academy of Fine Arts, Temple University, and Studio School of Art and Design, all in Philadelphia. He also attended a wide variety of marketing and advertising seminars and the School of Visual Arts in New York for a course in television production and direction. He has held several high-ranking positions in marketing, advertising, and sales and is founder and president of Creative Decisions of New York.

Edward's career began in 1961. After twelve years of working as designer, assistant art director, art director, and creative director, a freelance opportunity presented itself and he formed Ed Pitkoff Studios, which expanded and evolved into Creative Decisions, Inc., in 1973. He was attracted to the idea of producing high-quality creative advertising that could persuade a consumer to purchase a product. He credits a mentor who taught him "to marry the communication to the consumer so that the buyer could visualize themselves as part of the product."

Edward's advice to those interested in this field involves focus. "Don't ever become distracted," he says. "Always keep your focus on the business of advertising. And remember, what you might want to say to sell this product or service really isn't important. The only thing that is important is what would be compelling to the consumers. What do they want to hear? What do they want to buy? Ultimately, it is the consumers who judge how well your message has come across. If the product sells, then you know your focused communication has reached its audience."

Cliff Allen, Advertising and Public Relations Company Owner

Cliff Allen is the owner of Cliff Allen Consulting, a company that provides marketing for growing companies. He is the coauthor of two books, *Web Catalog Cookbook* and *One-to-One Web Marketing*, now in its second edition. He also writes articles about Web marketing, covering such topics as personalization, e-mail marketing, and marketing databases. He has written a weekly column on precision marketing for *ClickZ.com* and articles for other marketing publications.

Although he initially worked toward an engineering degree, Cliff became interested in computers and switched his college studies to business. He earned a bachelor of arts in marketing from the University of Tulsa in Oklahoma. After working in radio and television for nine years, he wanted to become an entrepreneur and started a software company designed to analyze radio and television ratings data. Although the business was not a huge success, Cliff learned a lot about remote computing, which was extremely useful to him in the next phase of his career.

Over the next thirteen years, Cliff worked for United Telecom and General Electric in software development, sales, and marketing of remote computing services. These jobs taught him a lot about the Internet, which was still fairly new.

In 1986, Cliff started Allen Marketing Group, an advertising and public relations firm that assisted software, hardware, and data communications companies with their marketing needs. Once the focus shifted primarily to the Internet, the company name was changed to Allen Interactive. In 1995 the company's line of Web personalization products was released, and in 1999 it released one of the first personalized e-mail products.

Before reorganizing the company, Cliff spent much of his day working with staff to ensure that they had the current skills and knowledge needed to keep up with the changing Internet environment. He also spent a significant amount of time working on sales and seeking out new projects, in addition to handling administrative functions and working directly with clients. Once the type of Web projects that the company handles began to evolve, Cliff reorganized with fewer employees and created an environment in which the entire staff could work independently from their homes. He credits this reorganization with improving company morale and the quality of his team's work.

Cliff works about fifty to sixty hours per week, which is not uncommon among executives in the Internet industry. "Of course, for me, working with the Internet is enjoyable," he says, "and part of my time on the Net is just for fun. It's a great feeling to share what I've learned about how to use the Internet to achieve a set of goals. Working directly with clients is very satisfying. Handling administrative functions and providing resources for the organization has its own set of rewards, but I don't find it as rewarding as working with clients."

Cliff's advice to others interested in this field is to start working for a small company that can provide experience in different areas of the industry. This can be a stepping-stone to working for a larger company, where you can focus on a few specialized areas. He recommends reading trade magazines to keep up with trends and the people who set them.

"Meet as many people as you can, both within your company and in the industry," Cliff advises. "Use a top-notch database to record your contacts. It's always amazing when someone you met years ago calls you out of the blue. You thus need a way to quickly recall information about them. Speak in front of groups whenever possible, whether it's a departmental meeting where you summarize your team's progress or an industry conference. People who stand up and speak are remembered and are seen as experts and leaders."

Dennis Abelson, Marketing and Advertising Professional

Dennis Abelson earned a bachelor of arts degree in classical languages from Washington University in St. Louis, Missouri, and a master of science in journalism with a focus on advertising from Northwestern University Medill School of Communications in Evanston, Illinois. He has experience as a copywriter, associate creative director, and creative director.

Dennis was working as a freelance writer but grew tired of the isolation and wanted more lucrative creative challenges. He was approached by someone who had seen one of his promotional mailings, and together they started a full-service marketing, consulting, and communications firm. After a slow start, the company began to grow and become more successful. Dennis and his partner changed their corporate name to Matrix Partners.

The company provides services such as packaging, advertising, promotion, direct mail, and sales presentations. Their clients include a distributor of computer cabling and networking systems; an agricultural biotechnology company, a manufacturer of diving equipment, and several food vendors.

"I originally got into the creative end of advertising because I couldn't see myself holding down a nine-to-five job," Dennis says. "It also gave me the opportunity to keep pursuing my interests in audio engineering and cartooning. In my undergraduate years, I was program director of the campus radio station as well as the creator of a weekly comic strip in the campus paper."

While Dennis says that there is not a typical day in his business, an average day might include these duties: revising ad copy, attending project status meetings, finalizing ad copy and sending it to the client, reviewing logo designs for a new account, performing online trademark search for a proposed line, eating lunch while working on a presentation, taking calls from clients, working with designers and writers on projects, editing presentations, and writing a direct mailer. In Dennis's estimation, this day would end at about 11 P.M.

"What does it mean to be doing my kind of work?" asks Dennis. "At times it seems totally thankless, but in what other profession do you get paid to legally hallucinate, to play creatively with concepts and pictures?"

Among the upsides of his work, Dennis lists a lack of corporate politics or hidden agendas, the opportunity to gain knowledge about many different industries, and the satisfaction of contributing to the success of a client's business.

On the other hand, the downsides include the long hours, difficult clients, and logistical and budgetary constraints on creativity.

Dennis offers this advice about his career: "I would tell others who are considering a career in advertising and marketing to start with the largest organization that will hire you. And be prepared for the long haul."

Jane Ward, Senior Marketing Specialist

Jane Ward received a bachelor of arts degree from Catholic University in Washington, D.C., where she majored in English with minors in French and philosophy. She later earned a master of philosophy degree in Irish Literature from Trinity College in Dublin, Ireland.

Jane had difficulty finding a job when she returned to the United States from Ireland in 1995. Without much work experience, her master's degree was more of a hindrance than a help in the job market. She learned Web publishing, including HTML conversion and layout, and found a well-paying job that utilized those skills. Although Jane found the work very boring and hoped to find a more interesting job, she was promoted twice.

Jane ultimately found a satisfying job as a marketing specialist with a software company, where she works creating public relations and marketing materials. She has been promoted to senior marketing specialist.

Jane writes website content and manages the site by supervising the graphic designers and approving graphics for the Web. She is in charge of press releases and ad copy and supervises ad production. She also attends several trade shows each year, staffing the booth or speaking to the press about the company where she works. Although she doesn't do any technical writing, she does help with product documentation by editing for style and grammar.

Jane works about fifty hours a week and often brings work home. "This is both good and bad," she says. "It provides a convenience, but sometimes I feel as if work has invaded my home life too much. I'm very busy, but the work environment is pretty relaxed with a very deliberate casualness. In software, people often wear very casual clothes and look down on typical corporate types who wear suits and work in the big city. Also, software, as an industry, is still very young. This is evidenced by the fact that the average age of people working for my company is probably less than thirty years."

When asked about what she likes and dislikes about her job, Jane says, "I enjoy writing a piece, a press release for example, and then seeing it picked up and published by a magazine. It gives me a thrill to see such immediate results from my work. But I don't like going to trade shows because I don't enjoy traveling and having to spend time away from my family. Also, that can get pretty tedious. However, I do understand that it's important for our company to be seen at important shows."

Jane's advice for anyone considering this type of career is to develop critical observation skills and learn to analyze advertisements to determine the goal of the people who created it, their target market, and the elements that went into creating the ad. She also recommends honing your writing skills. "I've seen so many graduates—even those of Ivy League schools—who can't write a complete sentence," she says. "And I strongly recommend a liberal arts education, which teaches you how to think and how to articulate your thoughts. These are the kinds of tools that you need to achieve success in any industry."

George DiDomizio, Advertising and Trademark Specialist

George DiDomizio is self-employed as president of Gemini Trademark Services in Pennsylvania. He earned a bachelor of business administration degree from Ursinus College in Pennsylvania after attending night school for ten years. He is pursuing a juris doctor degree from LaSalle University in Louisiana.

George worked in advertising for thirty-five years and began Gemini Trademark Services in 1992, after retiring from Merck and Company. Much of his time at Merck was spent working with trademark issues, and he served on the Merck Trademark Committee, which held brainstorming sessions in an effort to come up with trademarks for the company's products. "I enjoyed the process of 'making up language,'" George says, "and colleagues told me I had a knack for coming up with interesting and useful names."

George was promoted to director of creative services and asked to serve as chairperson of the Merck Trademark Committee. The trademark function was considered an addition to his regular advertising duties, which involved supervising an internal team of about thirty people and a group of about fifty outside agencies, design shops, film producers, and various other communication firms.

George devoted a lot of attention to the trademark committee, partly because he was attracted by the durability of trademarks. Although advertising campaigns and slogans have a limited life span, a trademark can last forever and grow more powerful and valuable with use. He found this an exciting aspect of the job and gave names to many of the company's most famous products, including the drugs Zocor and Pepcid AC.

George cites songwriting as the most important influence on his trademark work. He was among the founding members of Songwriters of North America (SONA), an organization that helps amateur songwriters to write, get their songs into print, obtain air time, and interest the press. George sees creating trademarks as similar to writing songs because both activities involve relating a message through a few words or letters. As George says, "Both a song and a trademark have the potential to become embedded in people's minds. Both a song and a trademark can evoke emotions."

George describes creating trademarks as playing with the alphabet, as he tries to come up with the six or seven letters that might best name a product. Most trademark projects involve long lists of potential candidates, sometimes more than a thousand, which are created through a variety of techniques, including brainstorming sessions and computer software programs.

"I like to work with a creative technique I call 'brain writing' that involves a group of six to fifteen people silently building on each other's ideas," George says. "We have a special form that participants use to enter their ideas for trademarks in a burst of three at a time. The form is passed along to another person, who is asked to build on the first three names or use any portion of the suggestions to come up with entirely new approaches. In a typical session of about thirty minutes, each person can generate about fifty candidates."

George also uses a software program called GENIX to generate trademark possibilities. It allows the user to create word fragments called phonemes that can be combined in an infinite variety of ways. "The easy part is building long lists of names," George says. "The hard part is sorting through the lists to find the linguistic gold. Using creative magic to generate the sequence of letters that forms a new word and meets the project criteria, then getting a legal green light for global availability is like hitting a grand slam."

About half of George's job is spent on the creative aspect, and another 20 to 30 percent is spent on legal aspects, assuring that potential trademark names are not already in use by others. A typical day for George begins with a walk with his dog. While this might seem like a routine task, for George it is his private brainstorming time, when he often comes up with insights and ideas for creative or legal challenges. By 7 A.M. he is in contact with European clients, and he tries to spend a few hours each morning on creative activities for new trademarks. The balance of the day is spent on conference calls, correspondence, the Internet, and related activities.

For George, the most enjoyable part of the job is creating language. "There is a wonderful satisfaction in knowing that a piece of language did not exist until you gave it form," he says. "Another positive part of my trademark adventure is being an expert in a very narrow field of commerce. The more difficult the challenge, the better I like it.

"I think that an ideal trademark person is one who knows more about trademark law than any marketing person and more about marketing than any trademark attorney."

For More Information

The following list includes professional associations and directories that can aid in your job search. Many of the publications are available in public libraries.

The American Marketing Association is a professional society of marketing and market research executives, sales and promotion managers, advertising specialists, academics, and others interested in marketing. The association fosters research; sponsors seminars, conferences, and student marketing clubs; and provides a placement service. It also offers a certification program for marketing managers and publishes the *Journal of Marketing*, *Journal of Marketing Research*, *Journal of Health Care Marketing*, and an international membership directory. For more information, contact:

American Marketing Association
311 South Wacker Drive, Suite 5800
Chicago, IL 60606
www.marketingpower.com

Members of the National Council for Marketing and Public Relations are communications specialists working within community, technical, and junior colleges in areas including alumni, community, government, media, and public relations as well as marketing, publications, and special events. The association works to foster improved relations between two-year colleges and their communities throughout the United States and Canada. The association holds an annual conference with exhibits, national surveys, and needs assessments and publishes a newsletter called "Counsel." For information, contact:

National Council for Marketing and Public Relations
PO Box 336039
Greeley, CO 80633
www.ncmpr.org

Sales and Marketing Executives International offers a management certification program. For information, contact:

Sales and Marketing Executives International
PO Box 1390
Sumas, WA 98295
www.smei.org

CHAPTER FOUR

Careers in Politics

Political action is the highest responsibility of a citizen.
—John F. Kennedy

HELP WANTED: FULL-TIME ASSISTANT TO VILLAGE MANAGER

Our small village is seeking an assistant for our busy village manager. We are interested in someone who can handle a variety of projects and details simultaneously. We need an individual with a college degree who has experience and a sustained interest in politics, government, and serving the public.

D oes a political job hold some interest for you? Are you attracted to the idea of serving others? Then read on for ideas on how you might find your niche in the world of politics.

Careers in Politics

At the top of the political hierarchy are public office holders, including mayors, governors, supervisors, senators, representatives, and, of course, the president and vice president of the country. All of these individuals are elected to administer government. They handle all of the business of a city, town, state, county, or the country as a whole. They must pass laws to keep order, set up special programs to benefit people, and spend the taxpayers' money on goods and services. As problem solvers, they meet with community leaders to determine the needs of the people, and then they search for ways to meet those needs.

There are many levels of political careers—all the way down to the local levels, including those who work informally for political change in their neighborhoods and those who work in an official capacity, such as precinct captain. Some of these jobs are voluntary, unpaid positions that could eventually lead to paying positions. All positions except appointed government managers are elected by their constituents. Nonelected managers are hired by a local government council or commission.

Chief Executives and Legislators

Government chief executives, like their counterparts in the private sector, have overall responsibility for the operation of their organizations. Working with legislators, they set goals and arrange programs to attain them. They appoint department heads to oversee the civil servants who carry out programs enacted by legislative bodies. Chief executives in government oversee budgets and ensure that resources are used properly and that programs are carried out as planned.

The duties of government chief executives also include meeting with legislators and constituents to determine the level of support for proposed programs. In addition, they often nominate citizens to boards and commissions, encourage business investment, and promote economic development in their communities. To do all these varied tasks effectively, chief executives of large governments rely on a staff of highly skilled aides to research issues that concern the public. Executives who control small governmental bodies, however, often do this work by themselves.

Legislators are elected officials who develop, enact, or amend laws. They include United States senators and representatives; state senators and representatives; and county, city, and town commissioners and council members.

Legislators introduce, examine, and vote on bills to pass official legislation. In preparing such legislation, they study staff reports and hear testimony from constituents, representatives of interest groups, board and commission members, and others with an interest in the issue under consideration. They usually must approve budgets and the appointments of nominees for leadership posts whose names are submitted by the chief executive. In some bodies, the legislative council appoints the city, town, or county manager.

Both chief executives and legislators perform many ceremonial duties, such as opening new buildings, making proclamations, welcoming visitors, and leading celebrations. It is both a privilege and an important responsibility to serve in public office.

Serving at State or Local Levels

Politically minded persuasive types may seek the following offices at the state and local levels:

Governor	County Clerk
Lt. Governor	Recorder
Secretary of State	Sheriff
State Senator	Treasurer
State Representative	Township Supervisor
State Treasurer	City/Village Manager
Attorney General	Board Secretary
Comptroller	Deputy Village Clerk
County Board President	City/Village Trustee
County Commissioner	Chief Librarian
Assessor	Parks Director
Clerk of the Circuit Court	Superintendent of Schools

State and local governments provide their constituents with vital services, such as transportation, public safety, health care, education, utilities, and courts. Excluding education and hospitals, state and local governments employ about 7.9 million workers, placing them among the largest employers in the economy. Around two-thirds of these employees work for local governments, such as counties, cities, special districts, and towns.

In addition to the 50 state governments, there are about 87,500 local governments, according to the U.S. Census Bureau. These include about 3,000 county governments, 19,400 municipal governments, 16,500 townships, 13,500 school districts, and 35,100 special districts. Illinois had the most local government units, with more than 6,900; Hawaii had the fewest, with 20.

In many areas of the country, citizens are served by more than one local government unit. For example, most states have counties, which may contain various municipalities, such as cities or towns, but which also often include unincorporated rural areas. Townships, which often contain suburban or rural areas, may include municipalities. Supplementing these forms of local government, special district government bodies are independent, limited-purpose governmental units that usually perform a single function or activity. For example, a large percentage of special districts manage the use of natural resources. Some provide drainage and flood control, irrigation, and soil and water conservation services.

Working Conditions

Opportunities for government or political jobs may be found throughout the country. The working conditions of chief executives and legislators vary with the size and budget of the governmental unit. Time spent at work ranges from meeting once a month for a local council member to sixty or more hours per week for a U.S. senator.

U.S. senators and representatives, governors and lieutenant governors, and chief executives and legislators in large local jurisdictions usually work full-time year-round, as do county and city managers. Many state legislators work full-time while legislatures are in session (usually for two to six months a year) and part-time the rest of the year. Local elected officials in many jurisdictions work a schedule that is officially designated part-time but actually is the equivalent of a full-time schedule when unpaid duties are taken into account.

In addition to their regular schedules, chief executives are on call at all hours to handle emergencies. Some jobs require occasional out-of-town travel, but others involve long periods away from home to attend sessions of the legislature.

Qualifications and Training

Voters seek to elect the individual believed to be most qualified from among a number of candidates who meet the minimum age, residency, and citizenship requirements. While there are no formal educational requirements for public officeholders, successful candidates must be able to show voters that they are qualified for the jobs they seek, and a good education is one of the best qualifications a candidate can offer.

Successful candidates usually have a strong record of accomplishment in paid and unpaid work in their districts. Some have business, teaching, or legal experience; others come from a wide variety of occupations. In addition, many have experience as members of boards or commissions.

Some candidates become well known for their work with charities, political action groups, political campaigns, or religious, fraternal, and social organizations.

Management-level work experience and public service help develop the planning, organizing, negotiating, motivating, fundraising, budgeting, public speaking, and problem-solving skills needed to run an effective political campaign. Candidates must make decisions quickly, sometimes on the basis of limited or contradictory information. They must inspire and motivate their constituents and their staffs. They need to appear sincere and candid and able to present their views thoughtfully and convincingly. Additionally, they must know how to hammer out compromises and satisfy the demands of constituents. National and statewide campaigns require massive amounts of energy and stamina, as well as superior fund-raising skills.

Town, city, and county managers are generally hired by the local council or commission. Managers come from a variety of educational backgrounds. A master's degree in public administration, including courses such as public financial management and legal issues in public administration, is widely recommended. Virtually all town, city, and county managers have at least bachelor's degrees, and the majority hold master's degrees. Working in management support positions in government is a prime source for the experience and personal contacts required in eventually securing a position as manager.

Generally, a town, city, or county manager in a smaller jurisdiction is required to have expertise in a wide variety of areas. Those who work for larger jurisdictions specialize in financial, administrative, and personnel matters. For all managers, communication skills and the ability to get along with others are essential.

Advancement opportunities for elected public officials are not clearly defined. Because elected positions normally require a period of residency and local public support is critical, officials can usually advance to other offices only in the jurisdictions where they live. For example, council members may run for mayor or for positions in the state government, and state legislators may run for governor or for Congress. Many officials are not politically ambitious, however, and do not seek advancement. Others lose their bids for reelection or voluntarily leave the occupation. A lifetime career as a government chief executive or legislator is rare except for those who reach the national level.

Town, city, and county managers have better-defined career paths. They generally obtain master's degrees in public administration, then gain experience as management analysts or assistants in government departments working for committees, councils, or chief executives. They learn about planning, budgeting, civil engineering, and other aspects of running a government. With sufficient experience, they may be hired to manage small governments and often move on to manage progressively larger governments over time.

Salaries

Earnings of public administrators vary widely, depending on the size of the government unit and on whether the job is part-time, full-time and year-round, or full-time for only a few months a year. Salaries range from little or nothing for a small town council member to $400,000 a year for the president of the United States.

The National Conference of State Legislatures reports that the annual salary for rank-and-file legislators in the forty states that paid an annual salary ranged from $10,000 to more than $99,000 in 2004. In eight states, legislators received a daily salary plus an additional allowance for living expenses while legislatures were in session. The Council of State Governments reports in its *Book of the States, 2002–2003* that gubernatorial annual salaries ranged from $50,000 in American Samoa to $179,000 in New York. In addition to a salary, most governors receive benefits such as transportation and an official residence.

In 2005, U.S. senators and representatives earned $162,100, the senate and house majority and minority leaders earned $180,100, and the vice president was paid $208,100.

Median annual earnings of local legislators were $15,220 in 2002. The middle 50 percent earned between $13,180 and $38,540. The lowest 10 percent earned less than $12,130, and the highest 10 percent earned more than $69,380.

The International City/County Management Association (ICMA) reported the 2004 median annual salaries of selected executive and managerial occupations in local government as follows:

City manager	$88,695
Assistant chief administrative officer	$80,232
Information services director	$75,582
Engineer	$75,556
Chief financial officer	$74,867
Economic development director	$70,668
Public works director	$70,135
Fire chief	$70,000
Human resources director	$70,000
Chief law enforcement official	$69,837
Human services director	$64,832
Parks and recreation director	$62,988
Health officer	$61,536
Purchasing director	$59,013
Chief librarian	$56,270
Treasurer	$52,053
Clerk	$46,779

Words from the Pros

If you think that a career in politics might suit your persuasive nature, read the following accounts to see whether these political careers might be right for you.

Margo Vroman, Assistant City Attorney

Margo Vroman is assistant city attorney in Lansing, Michigan. She is also a part-time adjunct professor at Michigan State University, Detroit College of Law. Margo earned her bachelor of science and master of arts degrees from Western Michigan University in Kalamazoo and her juris doctorate from the University of Toledo in Ohio.

Margo has been practicing law since 1982 and has worked with the city attorney's office since 1997, pursuing a career that combines litigation with appellate practice. She has always worked as a lawyer or legal writer, following a fairly diverse career. After trying private practice and working as a legal editor for a major publisher and for the Michigan Supreme Court, she decided that she liked best a job that combines diverse practical areas with the opportunity to write appellate court briefs.

She has been interested in being an attorney since childhood, when she formed an idealistic view of the law after watching the film *To Kill a Mockingbird*. Although practice experience has taught her that integrity and justice are not always the norm, Margo is rewarded on those occasions when she can help to right even a small wrong in another's life.

Margo is the chief appellate counsel in the civil division of the Lansing City Attorney's Office. As such, she works on all appeals filed or responded to by the office. For complicated cases, she coordinates a team of attorneys. Appellate work involves reading trial court transcripts, researching legal issues surrounding perceived legal errors, and writing a persuasive brief to convince the higher court of the validity of your position. The work includes a lot of time spent at the computer and in the law library. "It's not particularly stressful," Margo says, "unless there are numerous cases with simultaneous deadlines or you know the outcome can cost your client $15 million if you lose."

Margo also provides legal advice to city departments, the office of the mayor, and the city council. This can involve anything from having a brief conversation to preparing a written memo. In contract work, Margo specializes in software purchase agreements and handles most of her office's technology-related projects. She also litigates civil cases in state and federal court, which involves deposing witnesses, obtaining evidence, and preparing all pleadings, in addition to appearing in court.

According to Margo, at times her office is extremely busy, and it seems as though the staff cannot possibly complete everything that must be done. At other times the pace slows down, but generally the pace is somewhere in between.

When asked what she likes most about her position, Margo cites the diversity of her responsibilities. "I admittedly have a very short attention span and am easily bored," she says. "This job is good because I am always learning something new and am sometimes given the opportunity to present new and important legal issues to the Supreme Court. Every now and then, I get to feel as if my contribution actually makes a positive difference in the way things work."

Of course, not everything about the job is positive. "The downside of a position like this is that lawyers and law departments are always everyone's favorite whipping posts," Margo says. "When you tell people they can't legally do what they want to do, they respond by taking it out on the messenger. If they do it anyway and a lawsuit ensues, they blame the law department for not doing a good job. Also, when you work for a government entity, you always have to deal with the political ramifications of everything you do (not that this isn't a problem in other environments, too). As if this isn't enough, you also have to deal with the crazies who think it is their God-given right to show up in any governmental office and harass the people working there."

Margo's advice for anyone contemplating a career in law is to think it through very carefully. The cost of a legal education often outweighs the salary you can expect to earn as a lawyer. In addition, she says, "They had better make sure they have thick skin. You don't get many thank-yous in this business, but you do get a lot of blame and name-calling. Still, it's rewarding to know that, as a lawyer, you really can make a difference in this world."

Vera Marie Badertscher, Political Campaign Manager and Consultant

Vera Marie Badertscher earned both a bachelor of arts and a bachelor of science degree in education from Ohio State University in 1960. She went on to obtain a master of fine arts from Arizona State University in 1976, focusing on theater. Early in her career,

Vera worked primarily as a campaign manager but later became a campaign consultant. She currently works as a freelance writer.

Vera started as a citizen volunteer in city projects. As a young mother, she wanted a better library system in her town of Scottsdale, Arizona, so she volunteered for a committee. She met public officials, was invited to serve on their advisory committees, and eventually won a paid position managing a city council election campaign.

Vera found that she enjoyed working in politics, relishing both the sense of accomplishment and the ability to promote her beliefs and make things happen. She liked working with others who are action oriented and optimistic and says that her chief asset was the ability to figure out the best way to communicate political messages and move people to action.

Vera did volunteer work in a federated women's club, where she gained valuable experience, including "bringing diverse people together to work on projects, combining government and private energies, communicating, and organizing projects. My theater background helped me focus on short-term, collaborative projects."

As a campaign manager, Vera spent most of her working time communicating with volunteers, either by telephone or in memos and newsletters. The limited time of a political campaign makes the job very intense, and quick decision-making becomes a vital part of a campaign manager's duties. She says, "Someone advised me when I managed my first congressional campaign that during the last couple of weeks of the campaign, I would be making a dozen decisions every hour, and one in twenty or so would be truly important."

In addition, a successful campaign manager must also be able to prioritize. It is important to know the difference between decisions that do not affect the outcome of an election and those that do.

Vera summarizes a campaign manager's responsibilities: "A campaign manager rounds up diverse interest groups, volunteers, the candidate and his or her family, advertising personnel, researchers, and fund-raisers. The key to being successful is keeping the focus on what will get the candidate elected and not allowing anyone in the campaign to draw the focus in another direction. You can expect to talk on the phone all day, check off on other people's work, and stay close to the candidate to keep him or her on track. Generally, you are trying to keep costs down, so the work surroundings are on the primitive side—borrowed furniture and unpainted walls. You can count on noise and constant activity. (If it's quiet, you're probably losing.) This presents a hard atmosphere to concentrate in, but that's the job."

The work of a campaign consultant, by contrast, is somewhat less hectic. A campaign consultant generally has more time to think about issues and concentrate than does a campaign manager. The consultant typically analyzes voting data history; studies the candidate, the opponent, and the voters; and writes a strategic plan for bringing the voters to support that candidate. While some consultants specialize in media or mail, Vera worked as a generalist, developing strategies and writing direct mail.

The consultant works in an office or home office and meets weekly or biweekly with the candidate, the campaign manager, and others involved in the campaign. Once the plan is written, the consultant is available to help fine-tune the campaign, make adjustments, review media plans, determine what to ask in polling, and interpret the results. While the campaign manager's job is not done until the polls close on election day, the consultant's job is done a few days prior to the election when no more mail can be sent or advertising launched that will affect the outcome.

Vera is frank about the aspects of her job that she likes and dislikes. She says, "I most like the ability to work out the puzzles involved in bringing together the circumstances, the candidate, and the voters in order to persuade them that they will be better off to elect that candidate. I like the thinking and the communicating of politics.

"What I least like is having to be nice to a bunch of people that I might not particularly like or admire. However, I have been fortunate in being able to choose the candidates I work for, so I have worked for people I believe in and personally support. However, politics is about coalition building, so sometimes the expression 'politics makes strange bedfellows' is all too true."

Vera offers this advice for aspiring campaign managers: "I would advise anyone interested in entering this kind of work to introduce yourself to a candidate you admire and volunteer to help. Political science classes teach theory, but only campaigning teaches campaigning. Don't try to tell the candidate how to run his or her campaign or volunteer to be the brains behind the organization until you have actually done some of the grunt work of campaigning and learned it from the inside out. You'd be surprised how many people come to a campaign manager and say, 'I'm really good at strategy,' when all the campaign manager really needs is someone to go out in a pickup truck and put up signs. And before any of that—register to vote. Read up on the issues. And, last but not least—vote!"

Wade Hyde, Political Consultant

Wade Hyde earned a bachelor of arts in education and history from East Texas State University in Commerce. He then received a master of arts in urban affairs from the University of Texas at Arlington and a master of arts in civic affairs teaching from the University of Dallas in Irving, Texas. He has served as a volunteer campaign consultant, as a civic volunteer board member, and as a planning and zoning commission member in Irving, Texas. Wade has also served as a member of the regional transportation board and member and officer of the Visiting Nurses Association.

In 1980, Wade began volunteering in organizations that supported interests with legislative agendas. He found that what interested him most were political events, including presidential nominating conventions, and the results of local elections.

"History studies and government were naturally interesting and easy for me," Wade says. "No other subject particularly intrigued me. Politics and policy are my calling."

Wade explains that there are differences among the types of political campaigns. The work is seasonal, although the type of campaign (local, regional, or national) determines whether the season lasts three months or two years. Local campaigns usually last about three months, so the job is very intense with the work concentrated into such a short length of time. In addition, many candidates in local elections know very little about such issues as fund-raising, coalition building, or voter lists, making the campaign manager's job even more stressful.

"The nature of the political candidate is usually one of tremendous energy and strong ego with an unshakable belief that the voting populace cannot live without his or her leadership," he says. "The consultant, on the other hand, must bring some order and a consistent, coherent message to the candidate and the workers. The atmosphere is one of chaotic, pressure-cooker days and nights."

Given the intensity of the work, it is not surprising that Wade would acknowledge some negative aspects of the job. As he says, "Everything is always late, unexpected, and includes last-minute and last-second decision making—sometimes like flipping a coin and forging ahead or backtracking. The days start as if the nights had never quit, and each workday lasts about eighteen hours. Both the candidate and campaign workers contract battle fatigue that doesn't end until weeks after election day. Saturdays and Sundays are not exempt."

Fortunately, there is a bright side to the challenges of being a political consultant. "Each new campaign and candidate comes with the promise of a better day and a better way. It's exciting and hopeful to be involved in making a positive change by helping elect someone who can make a big difference. At least that's the upside. The downside is the exhaustion and condensed pressure of a compact campaign effort and, if such should occur, the loss of the candidate's best effort."

Wade offers his view on how to prepare for campaign work: "I would advise others interested in entering this field to understand fully and honestly why you are working for a candidate. Know if you're primarily in it for a job, an appointment, for the experience and excitement, or for the candidate. Be realistic and don't hang around too long because burnout can set in quite soon. See *Wag the Dog* and *Primary Colors*—I found them to be pretty accurate as campaign compilations."

K. Mark Takai, State Representative

K. Mark Takai earned a bachelor of arts degree in political science in 1990 and a master of public health degree in health education in 1993 from the University of Hawaii at Manoa, Honolulu. During his internship for his master's degree, he worked for a council member for the city and county of Honolulu.

"My experiences at the University of Hawaii while an undergraduate student, graduate student, and employee probably attracted me to the state capitol," he says. "It was through these years that I had the most interaction with the legislators. I now serve as an elected state representative representing District 34, part of Aiea and part of Pearl City (both located near Pearl Harbor on Oahu)."

Mark became interested in elected office when he was involved in student government in fourth grade. This involvement continued through high school and college, where he served as student body president, representing twenty-four hundred students and twelve thousand students, respectively. He declared his candidacy for public office in July 1994, won the primary election in September, and was declared the winner of the seat after the general election in November.

"The job of a state representative runs the gamut," Mark says. "There are probably three different 'jobs' of an elected official—

very diverse, but all very important. The first is my job as a community leader. This is probably the most rewarding part of being in public office. The interaction with the community—through the schools, community organizations, neighborhood board meetings, and so forth—all provide me with the opportunity to listen and then respond to the desires and concerns of the public.

"This part of the job can also be very difficult. I have been very fortunate in that I have not had too many difficult meetings with the public; however, as a freeway project is currently being planned and the project calls for possible public condemnation of private property, I have had my fair share of angry constituents. Most times, though, I am able to work with the residents of our community to address their concerns.

"The second part of my job is as a lawmaker. Constitutionally, this is my most important responsibility. Seventy-five legislators decide what laws are passed.

"My third responsibility is as a politician (i.e., a political candidate). This is a very time-consuming process. The 'campaign season' begins around July of even-numbered years and doesn't end until the general election in early November. Aside from raising money to run a successful campaign (marketing materials, brochures, advertisements, and so forth), the most difficult and time-consuming tasks of the political season are sign waving— waving to cars along the roadside in the mornings and afternoons—and door-to-door canvassing." Since winning his first election in 1994, Mark has run five successful reelection campaigns for a two-year office.

Mark's typical workday depends on the time of year. During the legislative session, from January to May, he begins his day with a 7:30 A.M. breakfast meeting, followed by committee meetings at the state capitol beginning by 9 A.M. The legislators hold private meetings in their offices and catch up on phone calls and messages prior to the House floor session at noon. He eats lunch with constituents or attends a luncheon meeting after the floor session. Committee hearings begin at 2 P.M. and last until 7 P.M. The day usually ends with community meetings that run until about 10 P.M. Saturdays are generally spent at committee hearings or community events. Mark reserves Friday evenings and Sundays for time with his family.

The months when the legislature is not in session or he is not running a reelection campaign do not necessarily afford slow workdays. Mark generally works in his office planning for upcoming events. For example, he is state cochair of Hawaii's Children and Youth Month and state chair of Hawaii's Junior Miss Scholarship Program, both of which often find him even busier out of session than during the legislative session.

It is not surprising that this challenging career has its ups and downs. Mark describes his feelings about the job: "The period of nonsession months during the campaign season is really tough and grueling. And, including time spent at receptions, dinners, and so on, I probably spend about seventy hours a week working. However, the people I work with (both in the state capitol and throughout the community) make my job most rewarding. I would not trade the experiences that I have had for any other job. Although it can be very stressful and time-consuming, I truly enjoy my job as a state representative.

"I derive great pleasure from doing for others. For instance, one of my most rewarding moments occurred when I was able to provide assistance in getting funds to build a new traffic signal at an intersection that saw many near accidents, numerous accidents, and one fatality.

"The least enjoyable part of my job is knowing full well that every bill that we pass and that becomes law has a negative impact on someone or on a specific profession. Although I have voted for many bills that do much good for our community overall, sometimes it is these same bills that get people laid off from their jobs, and so forth. Knowing this causes me great pain."

Mark has some advice for those interested in running for public office: "I would encourage anyone interested in pursuing this kind of career to talk to people about what their concerns are.

Meet with various leaders in your community. Get involved with political campaigns and volunteer or work for an elected official. And if you are truly serious, begin your plans for an eventual run for public office. Good luck!"

For More Information

Information on appointed officials in local government can be obtained from:

International City/County Management Association
777 North Capitol Street NE, Suite 500
Washington, DC 20002
www.icma.org

Here are some additional resources:

Democratic National Committee
Young Democrats of America
430 South Capitol Street SE
Washington, DC 20003
www.democrats.org

Republication National Committee
310 First Street SE
Washington, DC 20003
www.rnc.org

The Congressional Management Foundation
513 Capitol Court NE, Suite 300
Washington, DC 20002
www.cmfweb.org

United States Office of Personnel Management
1900 E Street NW
Washington, DC 20415
www.opm.gov

USAJOBS
www.usajobs.opm.gov
> *USAJOBS is the federal government's official source for federal
> employment information. Visitors to the site can search thousands of
> federal jobs, create and submit a resume, and download forms.*

CHAPTER FIVE

Careers in Law

No man is above the law and no man is below it; nor do we ask any man's permission when we require him to obey it.

—Theodore Roosevelt

HELP WANTED: LAWYER

Our well-known law firm is seeking to hire another lawyer. Candidates must have five years of experience and all of the proper legal credentials to be practicing law in this state. We seek someone who is personable, capable, empathetic, and knowledgeable about both people and the law. Travel will be a necessary part of the job, so we need someone who can leave town on short notice when necessary. A future partnership is definitely a possibility.

If you're considering a career as a lawyer, you might be imagining a defense attorney like Mark Geragos or a district attorney like Jack McCoy from television's "Law and Order." Or you might have seen Perry Mason, the original television lawyer, in old black-and-white reruns. His clients were always innocent, he always got them off, and he always nabbed the real criminal to boot.

But real life doesn't always follow high-profile cases or the imagination of television writers. If criminal law is the area that interests you, you should know that many of your clients will not be innocent, and you might not be able to get them all off. Some you'd rather not even represent. But, in our justice system, everyone is innocent until proven guilty, and everyone is entitled to legal defense.

Lawyers

Areas of Specialty

Although criminal law is a very popular and much-publicized specialty, it is not the only avenue lawyers can pursue. The more detailed aspects of a lawyer's job depend on his or her field of specialization and position. Even though all lawyers are allowed to represent parties in court, some appear in court more frequently than others. Lawyers who specialize in trial work need an exceptional ability to think quickly and speak with ease and authority, and they must be thoroughly familiar with courtroom rules and strategy. But trial lawyers still spend most of their time outside the courtroom conducting research, interviewing clients and witnesses, and handling other details in preparation for trial.

Some attorneys may never see the inside of a courtroom. The majority of lawyers are in private practice, where they may concentrate on criminal or civil law. What follows is an overview of each type of law specialization.

Criminal Law. Criminal lawyers represent or prosecute people who have been charged with crimes. Their responsibility is to argue their clients' cases, or the state's case, in courts of law. These attorneys operate their own practices, work for private law firms, or represent clients under the auspices of the public defender's office.

Lawyers who work for state attorneys, general prosecutors, and courts play a key role in the criminal justice system. At the federal level, attorneys investigate cases for the Department of Justice or other agencies. Also, lawyers at every government level help develop programs, draft laws, interpret legislation, establish enforcement procedures, and argue civil and criminal cases on behalf of the government.

Civil Law. In civil law, attorneys assist clients with litigation, wills, trusts, contracts, mortgages, titles, and leases. Some manage personal property as trustees or, as executors, see that provisions of clients' wills are carried out. Others handle only public-interest cases, civil or criminal, that have a potential impact extending well beyond the individual client.

Other lawyers work for legal aid societies, which are private, nonprofit organizations that were established to serve disadvantaged people.

Some other specializations within civil law include:

bankruptcy	insurance law
probate	family law
international law	corporate law
environmental law	real estate law
intellectual property	tax law

Lawyers sometimes are employed full-time by a single client. If the client is a corporation, the lawyer is known as house counsel and usually advises the company about legal questions that arise from its business activities. These questions might involve patents, government regulations, contracts with other companies, property interests, libel issues, or collective-bargaining agreements with unions.

Among the institutions that employ house counsels are banks, large manufacturing companies, and publishing houses.

Government Attorneys. Attorneys employed at the various levels of government comprise another category of the field. The attorney general of any state is the chief law officer of the state. Under the attorney general, you will find hundreds of assistant attorneys general, or district attorneys, as they are often called, in offices in various cities throughout each state. Government attorneys represent the state in civil actions, such as the big tobacco lawsuits that surface in the news from time to time.

In some states, local prosecutors have an appellate division in each office, and these attorneys handle only appeals. Once in a while, one side or the other will request an oral argument, and then the appeals attorneys must go to court. If the verdict is overturned, the state often has to retry the case.

Law Clerks. *Law clerk* can be a misleading title. Many people mistakenly think it refers to someone who is an administrative assistant as opposed to an attorney. But law clerks are, indeed, attorneys. In recent years some have begun using the title *research attorney*, which might be a more fitting description of the position. Sometimes they're called elbow clerks because they work at the elbow of the judge, usually for a one- to two-year stint directly out of law school or, for some, as a full-time, professional career. Duties vary depending on the judge you work with, but in general reading briefs, writing notes on them, and conducting research are a law clerk's main responsibilities.

Law clerks must be highly qualified attorneys. Most have graduated in at least the top quarter or higher of their class. As a full-time career, a job as a law clerk has its pluses and minuses. Salaries are generally much lower than those paid by private law firms, and job security depends on whether the judge you work for stays on the bench. He or she could retire or fail to win reelection, which would mean the end of your job. In contrast, the hours are fairly normal, and the job usually involves less stress and competition than a position in a busy law firm.

Law Professors. A relatively small number of trained attorneys work in law schools. Most are faculty members who specialize in one or more subjects. Others serve as administrators. Some work full-time in nonacademic settings and teach part-time.

Working Conditions for Lawyers

Lawyers do most of their work in offices, law libraries, and courtrooms. They sometimes meet in clients' homes or places of business and, when necessary, in hospitals or prisons. Many lawyers travel to attend meetings, gather evidence, and appear before courts, legislative bodies, and other authorities.

Salaried lawyers in government and private corporations usually have structured work schedules. Lawyers who are in private practice may work irregular hours while conducting research, conferring with clients, or preparing briefs during nonoffice hours.

Lawyers often work long hours, and, of those who regularly work full-time, about half work fifty hours or more per week. They may face particularly heavy pressure when a case is being tried. Preparation for court includes keeping abreast of the latest laws and judicial decisions. Although legal work generally is not seasonal, the work of tax lawyers and other specialists may be an exception. Because lawyers in private practice often can determine their own workload and the point at which they will retire, many stay in practice well beyond the usual retirement age.

The Role of the Attorney

No matter the setting, whether acting as advocates or prosecutors, all attorneys interpret the law and apply it to specific situations. This requires research and communication abilities. Lawyers perform in-depth research into the purposes behind the applicable laws and into judicial decisions that have been applied to those laws under circumstances similar to those currently faced by the client.

Lawyers are increasingly using various forms of technology to perform many of their tasks more efficiently. Although all lawyers continue to use law libraries to prepare cases, some supplement conventional printed sources with computer sources, such as the Internet and legal databases. Software is used to search this legal literature automatically and to identify legal texts relevant to a specific case. In litigation involving many supporting documents, lawyers may use computers to organize and index material. Lawyers also utilize electronic filing, videoconferencing, and voice-recognition technology to share information more effectively with other parties involved in a case.

Training and Qualifications

To practice law in the courts of any state or other jurisdiction, an attorney must be licensed, or admitted to its bar, under rules established by the jurisdiction's highest court. All states require that applicants for admission to the bar pass a written bar examination; most states also require applicants to pass a separate written ethics examination. In some cases, lawyers who have been admitted to the bar in one state may be admitted to the bar in another without taking an examination if they meet the latter jurisdiction's standards of good moral character and a specified period of legal experience. In most cases, however, lawyers must pass the bar examination in each state in which they plan to practice. Federal courts and agencies set their own qualifications for those practicing before or in them.

To qualify for the bar examination in most states, an applicant usually must earn a college degree and graduate from a law school accredited by the American Bar Association (ABA) or the proper state authorities. ABA accreditation signifies that the law school, particularly its library and faculty, meets certain standards developed to promote quality legal education. As of 2005, there were 191 ABA-accredited law schools; others were approved by state authorities only. With certain exceptions, graduates of schools not approved by the ABA are restricted to taking the bar examination and practicing in the state or other jurisdiction in which the school is located; most of these schools are in California. In 2005, seven states—California, Maine, New York, Vermont, Virginia,

Washington, and Wyoming—accepted the study of law in a law office as qualification for taking the bar examination; three jurisdictions—California, the District of Columbia, and New Mexico —now accept the study of law by correspondence. Several states require registration and approval of students by the state Board of Law Examiners, either before the students enter law school or during their early years of legal study.

Although there is no nationwide bar examination, forty-eight states, the District of Columbia, Guam, the Northern Mariana Islands, Puerto Rico, and the Virgin Islands require the six-hour Multistate Bar Examination (MBE) as part of the overall bar exam; the MBE is not required in Louisiana or Washington. The MBE covers a broad range of issues, and sometimes a locally prepared state bar examination is given in addition to it. The three-hour Multistate Essay Examination (MEE) is used as part of the bar exam in several states. States vary in their use of MBE and MEE scores.

Many states also require Multistate Performance Testing (MPT) to test the practical skills of beginning lawyers. Requirements vary by state, although the test usually is taken at the same time as the bar exam.

In 2004, law school graduates in fifty-two jurisdictions were required to pass the Multistate Professional Responsibility Examination (MPRE), which tests their knowledge of the ABA codes on professional responsibility and judicial conduct. In some states, the MPRE may be taken during law school, usually after completing a course on legal ethics.

The required college and law school education usually takes seven years of full-time study after high school—four years of undergraduate study, followed by three years of law school. Law school applicants must have a bachelor's degree to qualify for admission. To meet the needs of students who can attend only part-time, a number of law schools have night or part-time divisions, which usually require four years of study; about one in ten graduates from ABA-approved schools attended part-time.

Although there is no prelaw major, prospective lawyers should develop proficiency in writing, speaking, reading, researching, analyzing, and thinking logically—all skills needed to succeed both in law school and in the profession. Regardless of major, a multidisciplinary background is recommended. Courses in English, foreign languages, public speaking, government, philosophy, history, economics, mathematics, and computer science are also useful. Students interested in a particular aspect of law may find related courses helpful. For example, prospective patent lawyers need a strong background in engineering or science, and future tax lawyers must have extensive knowledge of accounting.

Acceptance by most law schools depends on the applicant's ability to demonstrate an aptitude for the study of law, usually through good undergraduate grades, the Law School Admission Test (LSAT), the quality of the applicant's undergraduate school, any prior work experience, and sometimes a personal interview. However, law schools vary in the weight they place on each of these and other factors.

All law schools approved by the ABA require applicants to take the LSAT. Nearly all law schools require applicants to have certified transcripts sent to the Law School Data Assembly Service, which then submits the applicants' LSAT scores and their standardized records of college grades to the law schools of their choice. Both this service and the LSAT are administered by the Law School Admission Council. Competition for admission to many law schools, especially the most prestigious ones, is generally intense, with the number of applicants greatly exceeding the number that can be admitted.

Studies during the first year of law school usually include core courses, such as constitutional law, contracts, property law, torts, civil procedure, and legal writing. In the remaining time, students may take specialized courses in fields such as tax, labor, or corporate law. Law students often acquire practical experience by participating in school-sponsored legal clinics; in the school's moot court competitions, in which students conduct appellate arguments; in practice trials under the supervision of experienced lawyers and judges; and through research and writing on legal issues for the school's law journal.

A number of law schools have clinical programs in which students gain legal experience through practice trials and projects under the supervision of practicing lawyers and law school faculty. For example, law school clinical programs might include work in legal aid clinics or on the staff of legislative committees. Part-time or summer clerkships in law firms, government agencies, and corporate legal departments also provide valuable experience. Such training can lead directly to a job after graduation and can help students decide what kind of practice best suits them. Clerkships also may be an important source of financial aid.

Law school graduates receive the degree of juris doctor (J.D.) as the first professional degree. Advanced law degrees may be desirable for those planning to specialize, research, or teach. Some law students pursue joint degree programs, which usually require an additional semester or year of study. Joint degree programs are offered in a number of areas, including law and business administration or public administration.

After graduation, lawyers must keep informed about legal and nonlegal developments that affect their practices. Currently, forty states and jurisdictions mandate continuing legal education (CLE). Many law schools and state and local bar associations provide continuing education courses that help lawyers stay abreast of recent developments. Some states allow CLE credits to be obtained through participation in seminars on the Internet.

The practice of law involves a great deal of responsibility. Individuals planning careers in law should like to work with people and be able to win the respect and confidence of their clients, associates, and the public. Perseverance, creativity, and reasoning ability also are essential to lawyers, who often analyze complex cases and handle new and unique legal problems.

Advancement and Employment Outlook

Most beginning lawyers start in salaried positions, usually as associates, and work with more experienced lawyers or judges. After several years of gaining responsibilities, some lawyers are admitted to partnership in the firm or go into practice for themselves. Some experienced lawyers are nominated or elected to judgeships. Others become full-time law school faculty or administrators; a growing number of these lawyers have advanced degrees in other fields as well.

Some attorneys use their legal training in administrative or managerial positions in various departments of large corporations. A transfer from a corporation's legal department to another department often is viewed as a way to gain administrative experience and rise in the ranks of management.

Lawyers held about 735,000 jobs in 2004. Approximately three out of four lawyers practiced privately, either as partners in law firms or in solo practices. Most salaried lawyers held positions in government or with corporations or nonprofit organizations. The greatest number of government attorneys were employed at the local level. In the federal government, lawyers work for many different agencies but are concentrated in the departments of Justice, Treasury, and Defense.

Many salaried lawyers working outside of government are employed as house counsel by public utilities, banks, insurance companies, real estate agencies, manufacturing firms, and other business and nonprofit organizations. Some also have part-time independent practices, while others work part-time as lawyers and full-time in another occupation.

Employment of lawyers is expected to grow between 9 and 17 percent through 2014, primarily as a result of growth in the population and in the general level of business activities. Job growth among lawyers will also result from increasing demand for legal services in such areas as health care, intellectual property, venture capital, energy, environmental, antitrust, and elder law. In addition, the wider availability and affordability of legal clinics should result in increased use of legal services by middle-income people.

However, growth in demand for lawyers will be limited as businesses, in an effort to reduce costs, increasingly use large accounting firms and paralegals to perform some of the same functions that lawyers do. For example, accounting firms may provide employee-benefit counseling, process documents, or handle various other services previously performed by a law firm. Also, mediation and dispute resolution increasingly are being used as alternatives to litigation.

Given the large number of students who graduate from law schools each year, competition for job openings should continue to be strong. Graduates with superior academic records from highly regarded law schools will have the best job opportunities. Perhaps as a result of competition for attorney positions, lawyers are increasingly finding work in nontraditional areas for which legal training is an asset but not normally a requirement, such as administrative, managerial, and business positions in banks, insurance firms, real estate companies, government agencies, and other organizations. Employment opportunities are expected to continue to arise in these organizations at a growing rate.

As in the past, some graduates may have to accept positions in areas outside of their fields of interest or for which they feel overqualified. Some recent law school graduates who have been unable to find permanent positions are turning to the growing number of temporary staffing firms that place attorneys in short-term jobs until they are able to secure full-time positions. This service allows companies to hire lawyers on an as-needed basis and permits beginning lawyers to develop practical skills while looking for permanent positions.

Because of the stiff competition for jobs, a law graduate's work experience and geographic mobility assume greater importance. However, while willingness to relocate may be an advantage in getting a job, a lawyer may have to take an additional state bar examination in order to be licensed to practice in a different location. In addition, employers are increasingly seeking graduates who have advanced law degrees and experience in a specialty, such as tax, patent, or admiralty law.

Employment growth for lawyers will continue to be concentrated in salaried jobs, as businesses and all levels of government employ a growing number of staff attorneys and as employment in the legal services industry grows. Most salaried positions are in urban areas where government agencies, law firms, and big corporations are concentrated.

The number of self-employed lawyers is expected to decrease slowly, reflecting the difficulty of establishing a profitable new practice in the face of competition from larger, established law firms. The growing complexity of law, which encourages specialization, along with the cost of maintaining up-to-date legal research materials, also favors larger firms.

For lawyers who wish to work independently, establishing a new practice will probably be easiest in small towns and expanding suburban areas. Competition from larger, established law firms is likely to be less keen than in big cities, and new lawyers may find it easier to become known to potential clients.

Some lawyers are adversely affected by cyclical swings in the economy. During recessions, demand declines for some discretionary legal services, such as planning estates, drafting wills, and handling real estate transactions. Also, corporations are less likely to litigate cases when declining sales and profits result in budgetary restrictions. Some corporations and law firms will not hire new attorneys until business improves, and these establishments may even cut staff to contain costs. Several factors, however, mitigate the overall impact of recessions on lawyers; during recessions, for example, individuals and corporations face other legal problems, such as bankruptcies, foreclosures, and divorces that require legal action.

Salaries

Law is a much more demanding profession than most people realize, and it is not always the high-income profession many people think it is. Yes, a lot of attorneys do earn a lot of money. But there are also attorneys running themselves ragged from courtroom to courtroom who barely earn enough to pay back their school loans.

Contrary to the experience of John Grisham's hero in *The Firm*, annual salaries of beginning lawyers in private industry average about $60,000. But, in some cases, top graduates from the nation's best law schools can start at more than $100,000 a year.

Factors affecting the salaries offered to new graduates include academic record; type, size, and location of employer; and the specialized educational background desired.

Here's a look at average annual salaries for new attorneys, just nine months after graduation, in a variety of specializations:

Private practice	$80,000
Business and industry	$60,000
Judicial clerkship or government	$44,700
Higher education	$40,000

Lawyers who own their own practices usually earn less than those who are partners in law firms. Lawyers starting their own practices may need to work part-time in other occupations to supplement their income until the practice is well established.

Most salaried lawyers are provided health and life insurance, and contributions are made to retirement plans on their behalf. Lawyers who practice independently are covered only if they arrange and pay for such benefits themselves.

Practicing Law in Canada

In Canada, the legal profession is a self-governing body, regulated in each province by a Law Society. The Law Society determines whether an applicant can be licensed to practice law. The basic procedure for a prospective lawyer is to graduate from an approved law school and complete the bar admission course in the province in which you want to practice.

The academic prerequisite for taking the bar admission course is either graduation from a common law program approved by the Law Society, in a university in Canada, or a certificate of qualification issued by the National Committee on Accreditation. There are sixteen universities in Canada that offer law courses approved by the Law Society. A student must meet the requirements of the university in order to study law. An approved law course takes three years to complete and leads to a bachelor of laws (LL.B.) or doctor of jurisprudence (J.D.) degree.

The specific requirements for the bar admission course differ among the provinces, but in general, the course is comprised of three phases: a skills phase, a substantive/procedural phase, and an articling phase. The skills and substantive/procedural phases usually run from eight to ten weeks each. The articling phase (the development of practical legal skills under the supervision of a lawyer) can last ten to twelve months. The bar examination is taken upon successful completion of the bar admission course. All lawyers must join the Law Society in the province where they practice.

. . . .

Paralegals

While lawyers assume ultimate responsibility for legal work, they often delegate many of their tasks to paralegals. In fact, paralegals, also called legal assistants, are continuing to assume a growing range of tasks in legal offices and perform many of the same tasks as lawyers. However, they are still explicitly prohibited from carrying out duties that are considered to be the practice of law, such as setting legal fees, giving legal advice, and presenting cases in court.

One of a paralegal's most important tasks is helping lawyers prepare for closings, hearings, trials, and corporate meetings. Paralegals investigate the facts of cases and ensure that all relevant information is considered. They also identify appropriate laws, judicial decisions, legal articles, and other materials that are relevant to assigned cases. After they analyze and organize the information, paralegals may prepare written reports that attorneys use in determining how cases should be handled. When attorneys decide to file lawsuits on behalf of clients, paralegals may help prepare the legal arguments, draft pleadings and motions to be filed with the court, obtain affidavits, and assist attorneys during trials. Paralegals also organize and track files of all important case documents and make them available and easily accessible to attorneys.

Paralegals perform a number of other vital functions in addition to this preparatory work. For example, they help draft contracts, mortgages, separation agreements, and instruments of trust. They also may assist in preparing tax returns and planning estates. Some paralegals coordinate the activities of other law office employees and maintain financial office records. Additional tasks may differ, depending on the employer.

Most paralegals are employed by law firms, corporate legal departments, and government offices. They can work in many different areas of the law, including litigation, personal injury, corporate law, criminal law, employee benefits, intellectual property, labor law, bankruptcy, immigration, family law, and real estate. As the law has become more complex, paralegals have responded by becoming more specialized. Within specialties, functions often are broken down further so that paralegals may deal with a specific area. For example, paralegals specializing in labor law may concentrate exclusively on employee benefits.

The duties of paralegals also differ widely with the type of organization in which they are employed. Paralegals who work for corporations often assist attorneys with employee contracts, shareholder agreements, stock-option plans, and employee benefit plans. They also may help prepare and file annual financial reports, maintain corporate minutes, record resolutions, and prepare forms to secure loans for the corporation. Paralegals often monitor and review government regulations to ensure that the corporation is aware of new requirements and is operating within the law. Increasingly, experienced paralegals are assuming additional supervisory responsibilities, such as overseeing team projects and serving as a communications link between the team and the corporation.

The duties of paralegals who work in the public sector usually vary within each agency. In general, paralegals analyze legal material for internal use, maintain reference files, conduct research for attorneys, and collect and analyze evidence for agency hearings. They may prepare informative or explanatory material on laws, agency regulations, and agency policy for general use by the agency and the public. Paralegals employed in community legal-service projects help the poor, the aged, and others who are in need of legal assistance. They file forms, conduct research, prepare documents, and, when authorized by law, may represent clients at administrative hearings.

Paralegals in small and medium-size law firms usually perform a variety of duties that require a general knowledge of the law. For example, they may research judicial decisions on improper police arrests or help prepare a mortgage contract. Paralegals employed by large law firms, government agencies, and corporations, however, are more likely to specialize in one aspect of the law.

As is the case with attorneys, familiarity with computers and technical knowledge has become essential to paralegal work. Computer software packages and the Internet are used to search legal literature stored in computer databases and on CD-ROM. In litigation involving many supporting documents, paralegals usually use computer databases to retrieve, organize, and index various materials. Imaging software allows paralegals to scan documents directly into a database, while billing programs help them to track hours billed to clients. Computer software packages also

are used to perform tax computations and explore the conse-
quences of various tax strategies for clients.

Training and Qualifications

There are several ways to become a paralegal. The most common
is through a community college paralegal program that leads to an
associate's degree. The other common method of entry, mainly for
those who already have a college degree, is through a program that
leads to a certification in paralegal studies. A small number of
schools also offer bachelor's and master's degrees in paralegal
studies. Some employers train paralegals on the job, hiring college
graduates with no legal experience or promoting experienced
legal secretaries. Other entrants have experience in a technical
field that is useful to law firms, such as a background in tax preparation for tax and estate practice or in criminal justice, nursing, or
health administration for personal injury practice.

An estimated one thousand colleges and universities, law
schools, and proprietary schools offer formal paralegal training
programs. Approximately 260 paralegal programs are approved by
the American Bar Association (ABA). Although many programs
do not require such approval, graduation from an ABA-approved
program can enhance one's employment opportunities. The
requirements for admission to these programs vary. Some require
certain college courses or a bachelor's degree; others accept high
school graduates or those with legal experience; a few schools
require standardized tests and personal interviews.

Paralegal programs include two-year associate's degree programs, four-year bachelor's degree programs, and certificate
programs that can take only a few months to complete. Most certificate programs provide intensive and, in some cases, specialized
paralegal training for individuals who already hold college degrees,
while associate's and bachelor's degree programs usually combine
paralegal training with courses in other academic subjects. The
quality of paralegal training programs varies; the better programs
usually include job placement services. Programs generally offer

courses introducing students to the legal applications of computers, including how to perform legal research on the Internet.

Many paralegal training programs also offer an internship in which students gain practical experience by working for several months in a private law firm, the office of a public defender or attorney general, a bank, a corporate legal department, a legal aid organization, or a government agency. Experience gained in internships is an asset when one is seeking a job after graduation. Prospective students should examine the experiences of recent graduates before enrolling in a particular program.

Although most employers do not require certification, earning a voluntary certificate from a professional society may offer advantages in the labor market. The National Association of Legal Assistants (NALA), for example, has established standards for certification that require various combinations of education and experience. Paralegals who meet these standards are eligible to take a two-day examination, given three times each year at several regional testing centers. Those who pass this examination may use the Certified Legal Assistant (CLA) designation. NALA also offers an advanced paralegal certification for those who want to specialize in other areas of the law. In addition, the Paralegal Advanced Competency Exam, administered through the National Federation of Paralegal Associations, offers professional recognition to paralegals with a bachelor's degree and at least two years of experience. Those who pass this examination may use the Registered Paralegal (RP) designation.

Paralegals must be able to document and present their findings and opinions to a supervising attorney. They need to understand legal terminology and have good research and investigative skills. Familiarity with the operation and applications of computers in legal research and litigation support is also important. Paralegals should stay informed of new developments in the laws that affect their area of practice. Participation in continuing legal education seminars allows paralegals to maintain and expand their knowledge of the law.

Because paralegals frequently deal with the public, they should be courteous and uphold the ethical standards of the legal profession. The National Association of Legal Assistants, the National Federation of Paralegal Associations, and a few states have established ethical guidelines for paralegals to follow.

Paralegals usually are given more responsibilities and require less supervision as they gain work experience. Experienced paralegals who work in large law firms, corporate legal departments, or government agencies may supervise and delegate assignments to other paralegals and clerical staff. Advancement opportunities also include promotion to managerial and other law-related positions within the firm or corporate legal department. However, some paralegals find it easier to move to another law firm when seeking increased responsibility or advancement.

Earnings for Paralegals

Earnings of paralegals and legal assistants vary greatly, depending on education, training, experience, the type and size of employer, and the geographic location of the job. In general, paralegals who work for large law firms or in large metropolitan areas earn more than those who work for smaller firms or in less populated regions. Many paralegals receive bonuses in addition to their salary.

In May 2004, full-time wage and salary paralegals and legal assistants had median annual earnings, including bonuses, of $39,130. The middle 50 percent earned between $31,040 and $49,950. The top 10 percent earned more than $61,390, while the bottom 10 percent earned less than $25,360. Median annual earnings in the industries employing the largest numbers of paralegals in May 2004 were as follows:

Federal government	$59,370
Local government	$38,260
Legal services	$37,870
State government	$34,910

. . . .

Words from a Pro

If you think your persuasive tendencies would help you in practicing law, read the following account to see whether you are right.

Nicole D. Blake, Attorney

Nicole D. Blake is a self-employed lawyer in Seattle, Washington. She received her bachelor of arts in political science from Loyola University in Chicago, then earned her juris doctor from DePaul University in Chicago.

Nicole has been a lawyer since 1991. "I always wanted to help others," she says. "I don't have a mathematical mind, but I do have a great ability and proclivity for argument, so it seemed an obvious career path. Also, I come from a family that stressed education. Several family members had already followed a career path in law. In fact, one of my cousins was the first blind lawyer admitted to practice in Chicago."

Nicole's first job after law school was working as a public defender. In this position, she worked in dependency law, which involved defending parents against losing their rights when the state has removed their children to foster care. The caseload was high, which made the job difficult. Following her work as a public defender, Nicole did some nonlegal work as an adoption social worker for a nonprofit agency. She worked at that job for about eighteen months before being laid off.

In her private practice, Nicole focuses mainly on dependency law and its related areas of divorce, adoption, and other aspects of family law. Her daily schedule is varied because something unexpected happens on most days. However, Nicole says that certain aspects of her day are constant. For instance, she spends a good deal of time returning calls. "I rarely answer the phone because this is one of the few ways that I can remain in charge of my own time," Nicole explains. "Another common responsibility is to attend hearings, often in more than one courthouse in more than one city at a time. Usually I work on at least one legal writing per day. Filing paperwork or figuring out what to do with any certain piece of paper is the time waster that I resent the most."

Nicole enjoys working with clients, especially when a case is going well. Things become difficult, however, when a client doesn't understand her role or the limitations of the law to resolve their issues.

"As a solo practitioner, I enjoy being my own boss, organizing my own schedule," Nicole says. "Then again, I dislike organizing my own schedule and keeping my own books."

Nicole advises anyone who is interested in practicing law to participate in debate teams in high school and college. Her final word of advice is this: "Study instead of going to parties so that you can get into one of the best possible law schools."

For More Information

The American Bar Association provides information about the law schools approved by the ABA, bar admissions requirements, and other information on legal education. To learn more, contact:

American Bar Association
321 North Clark Street
Chicago, IL 60610
www.abanet.org

For educational and career opportunities for attorneys in Canada, contact:

Canadian Bar Association
500–865 Carling Avenue
Ottawa, ON K1S 5S8
Canada
www.cba.org

Federation of Law Societies of Canada
Constitution Square
360 Albert Street, Suite 1700
Ottawa, ON K1R 7X7
Canada
www.flsc.ca

Information on the LSAT, the Law School Data Assembly Service, applying to law school, financial aid for law students, and law schools in the United States and Canada may be obtained from:

Law School Admission Council
www.lsac.org

General information on a career as a paralegal and a list of paralegal training programs approved by the American Bar Association is available from:

Division for Legal Services
American Bar Association
321 North Clark Street, Nineteenth Floor
Chicago, IL 60610
www.abanet.org/legalservices/paralegals/directory

For information on paralegal certification, training programs in specific states, and standards and guidelines, contact:

National Association of Legal Assistants
1516 South Boston, Suite 200
Tulsa, OK 74119
www.nala.org

For information on paralegal careers in Canada, contact the following:

Canadian Association of Paralegals
PO Box Station B
Montreal, QC H3B 3K5
Canada
www.caplegal.ca

CHAPTER SIX

Careers in Education

The foundation of every state is the education of its youth.
—Diogenes

S killed teachers know that the more persuasive they are about the benefits of education, the more children will learn. So, they use their persuasive skills to make learning interesting, challenging, and fun.

Educators Today

At the kindergarten and elementary school levels, teachers play a crucial role in children's development. What children learn and are exposed to during their early years can shape their views of themselves and of the world at large. Kindergarten and elementary school teachers introduce children to language, numbers, science, and social studies, establishing a foundation that can greatly affect later success or failure in school, work, and personal life.

At the elementary level, most teachers instruct one class of children in a variety of subjects. Sometimes two or three teachers work together or team teach. In other situations, a teacher may specialize in only one subject, such as art, music, science, reading, arithmetic, or physical education, or perhaps specialize in one area, such as special education or reading.

In some areas, teachers act as facilitators or coaches, using interactive discussions and hands-on learning to help pupils learn and apply the concepts involved in subjects like English, mathematics, or science. As teachers move away from the more traditional, repetitive drill and rote memorizing approaches to teaching, they are more likely to use manipulatives and props to help children solve problems, understand abstract concepts, and develop critical thought processes. Instead of the traditional flash cards, teachers may be more apt to use board games, computers, science apparatus, or tape recorders.

Working in group settings in order to discuss and solve problems is becoming more and more common. In this way, students are being prepared for future workforce situations. To be prepared for the long run, students must be able to interact with others, adapt to new technology, and logically think through their problems. Teachers can encourage the development of these skills by providing these learning opportunities.

Secondary school teachers help students delve more deeply into the subjects introduced in elementary school and also expose them to additional information about themselves and the world. Teachers at this level usually specialize in a particular subject, such as mathematics, biology, history, foreign languages, theater, or English. In some cases, instructors may teach more than one subject or may be involved in related subjects, such as American history, world history, and world geography.

At the college level, faculty members teach and advise students while conducting research, meeting with colleagues to keep up with developments in their fields, and consulting with government, business, nonprofit, and community organizations.

The Internet has provided a whole new world of opportunity for educators. Those with computer expertise may teach anything from individual classes on a wide variety of topics to regular college-credit courses through a number of colleges and universities. It is even possible to earn college degrees online.

The Role of the Educator

Teachers at the elementary and high school levels prepare classroom presentations and also work with students on a one-to-one basis. They plan, evaluate, and assign lessons; prepare, administer, and grade tests; and listen to oral presentations by the students. They observe and evaluate students' performances and increasingly use new assessment methods, such as portfolios, which judge a student's overall progress at the end of a learning period. Additional assistance is then provided in the needed areas.

Teachers also grade papers, prepare report cards, and meet with parents and school staff to discuss individual problems and student progress. Educators must also be adept at successfully maintaining classroom discipline.

In addition to classroom activities, some teachers oversee study halls and homeroom and supervise extracurricular activities. They identify physical or mental problems and refer students to the proper resource or agency for diagnosis and treatment. Secondary school teachers occasionally assist students in choosing courses, colleges, and careers. Teachers at all levels participate in educational conferences and workshops. In some school systems, teachers participate actively in management decisions regarding budgets, personnel, textbook choices, curriculum design, and teaching methods.

At the college level, teaching faculties are generally organized into departments or divisions, based upon subject or field. Professors often teach several different courses within their departments—English composition, fiction, and poetry, for example. They may work with undergraduate or graduate students or both. Classes may be in the form of large lecture sessions involving several hundred students, small seminars, or labs. Generally, professors are responsible for preparing lectures, exercises, and laboratory experiments; grading papers and exams; and advising individual students. Keeping abreast of developments in their field is an important aspect of their positions and, in most cases, educators are expected to experiment; collect and analyze data; examine original documents, literature, and other source material; develop hypotheses; arrive at conclusions; and publish their findings in scholarly journals, books, and electronic media.

Qualifications and Training

The required qualifications and training for teachers are very specific. In general, requirements vary depending on the grade level at which one hopes to teach.

Elementary and Secondary Education. All fifty states and the District of Columbia require public school teachers to be licensed. Licensure is not required for teachers in private schools in most states. Usually licensure is granted by the state Board of Education or a licensure advisory committee. Teachers may be licensed to teach the early childhood grades (usually preschool through grade three); the elementary grades (grades one through six or eight); the middle grades (grades five through eight); a secondary education subject area (usually grades seven through twelve); or a special subject, such as reading or music (usually kindergarten through grade twelve).

Although requirements for regular licenses to teach kindergarten through grade twelve vary by state, all states require general education teachers to have a bachelor's degree and to have completed an approved teacher training program with a prescribed number of subject and education credits, as well as supervised practice teaching. Some states also require technology training and the attainment of a minimum grade point average. A number of states require that teachers obtain a master's degree in education within a specified period after they begin teaching.

Almost all states require applicants for a teacher's license to be tested for competency in basic skills, such as reading and writing, and in teaching, as well as proficiency in his or her subject. Many school systems are presently moving toward implementing performance-based systems for licensure, which usually require a teacher to demonstrate satisfactory teaching performance over an extended period in order to obtain a provisional license, in addition to passing an examination in his or her subject. Most states require continuing education for renewal of the teacher's license. Many states have reciprocity agreements that make it easier for teachers licensed in one state to become licensed in another.

Many states also offer alternative licensure programs for teachers who have a bachelor's degree in the subject they will teach but who lack the necessary education courses required for a regular license. After working under the close supervision of experienced educators for one or two years while taking education courses outside school hours, they receive regular licensure if they have progressed satisfactorily. In other programs, college graduates who do not meet licensure requirements take only those courses that they lack and then become licensed. This approach may take one or two semesters of full-time study.

In many states, vocational teachers have many of the same requirements for teaching as their academic counterparts. However, because knowledge and experience in a particular field are important criteria for the job, some states will license vocational education teachers without a bachelor's degree, provided they can demonstrate expertise in the field. A minimum number of hours in education courses may also be required.

Licensing requirements for preschool teachers also vary by state. Requirements for public preschool teachers are generally more stringent than those for private preschool teachers. Some states require a bachelor's degree in early childhood education, while others require an associate's degree, and still others require certification by a nationally recognized authority. The Child Development Associate (CDA) credential, the most common type of certification, requires a mix of classroom training and experience working with children, along with an independent assessment of an individual's competence.

Private schools are usually exempt from meeting state licensing standards. For jobs teaching in secondary schools, the preference is generally for candidates who have a bachelor's degree in the subject they intend to teach. For elementary school teachers, a degree in childhood education is preferred. Private schools seek candidates among recent college graduates as well as from those who have established careers in other fields. Those schools associated with religious institutions also desire candidates who share the values that are important to the institution.

Postsecondary Education. Training requirements for postsecondary career and technical education teachers vary by state and by subject. In general, teachers need a bachelor's or higher degree, plus at least three years of work experience in the field. In some fields, a license or certificate that demonstrates one's qualifications may be all that is required. Teachers update their skills through continuing education in order to maintain certification. They must also maintain ongoing dialogue with businesses to determine the most current skills needed in the workplace.

Four-year colleges and universities usually consider doctoral degree holders for full-time, tenure-track positions but may hire master's degree holders or doctoral candidates for certain disciplines, such as the arts, or for part-time and temporary jobs. Most college and university faculty are in four academic ranks—professor, associate professor, assistant professor, and instructor—which are usually considered to be tenure-track positions. Most faculty members are hired as instructors or assistant professors. A smaller number of additional faculty members, called lecturers, are usually employed on contracts for a single academic term and are not on the tenure track.

In two-year colleges, master's degree holders fill most full-time positions. However, in certain fields where there may be more applicants than available jobs, institutions can be more selective in their hiring practices. In these fields, master's degree holders may be passed over in favor of candidates holding doctorates. Many two-year institutions increasingly prefer job applicants to have some teaching experience or experience with distance learning. Preference also may be given to those holding dual master's degrees, especially at smaller institutions, because they can teach more subjects.

Schools and programs that provide education and training for working adults generally hire people who are experienced in the field to teach part-time. A master's degree is also usually required.

Doctoral programs take an average of four to six years of full-time study beyond the bachelor's degree, including time spent completing a master's degree and a dissertation. Some programs, such as those in the humanities, may take longer to complete; others, such as those in engineering, usually are shorter. Candidates specialize in a subfield of a discipline—for example, organic chemistry, counseling psychology, or European history—but also take courses covering the entire discipline. Programs typically include twenty or more increasingly specialized courses and seminars plus comprehensive examinations on all major areas of the field.

Candidates also must complete a dissertation—a written report on original research in the candidate's major field of study that sets forth an original hypothesis or proposes a model and tests it. Students in the natural sciences and engineering usually do laboratory work; in the humanities, they study original documents and other published material. The dissertation is done under the guidance of one or more faculty advisors and usually takes one or two years of full-time work to complete.

Some students, particularly those who studied in the natural sciences, spend additional years after earning a degree on post-doctoral research and study before taking a faculty position. Some are able to extend postdoctoral appointments, or take new ones, if they are unable to find a faculty job. Most of these appointments offer a nominal salary.

Obtaining a position as a graduate teaching assistant is a good way to gain college teaching experience. To qualify, candidates must be enrolled in a graduate school program. In addition, some colleges and universities require teaching assistants to attend classes or take some training prior to being given responsibility for a course.

Although graduate teaching assistants usually work at the institution and in the department where they are earning their degrees, teaching or internship positions for graduate students at institutions that do not grant graduate degrees have become more common in recent years. For example, a program called Preparing Future Faculty, administered by the Association of American Colleges and Universities and the Council of Graduate Schools, has led to the creation of many now-independent programs that offer graduate students at research universities the opportunity to work as teaching assistants at other types of institutions, such as liberal arts or community colleges. Working with a mentor, the graduate students teach classes and learn how to improve their teaching techniques. They may attend faculty and committee meetings, develop a curriculum, and learn how to balance the teaching, research, and administrative roles that faculty play. These programs provide valuable learning opportunities for graduate students interested in teaching at the postsecondary level and also help to make these students aware of the differences among the various types of institutions at which they may someday work.

Certification and Advancement. In some cases, teachers of kindergarten through high school may attain professional certification in order to demonstrate competency beyond that required for a license. The National Board for Professional Teaching Standards offers a voluntary national certification. To become nationally accredited, experienced teachers must prove their aptitude by compiling a portfolio showing their work in the classroom and by passing a written assessment and evaluation of their teaching knowledge. Currently, teachers may become certified in a variety of areas on the basis of the age of the students and, in some cases, the subject taught. For example, teachers may obtain a certificate for teaching English language arts to early adolescents (aged eleven to fifteen), or they may become certified as early childhood generalists. All states recognize national certification, and many states and school districts provide special benefits to teachers holding such certification. Benefits typically include higher salaries and reimbursement for continuing education and certification fees. In addition, many states allow nationally certified teachers to carry a license from one state to another.

The National Council for Accreditation of Teacher Education currently accredits teacher education programs across the United States. Graduation from an accredited program is not necessary to become a teacher, but it does make it easier to fulfill licensure requirements. Generally, four-year colleges require students to wait until the sophomore year before applying for admission to teacher education programs. Traditional education programs for kindergarten and elementary school teachers include courses designed specifically for those preparing to teach. Courses include mathematics, physical science, social science, music, art, and literature, as well as prescribed professional education courses, such as philosophy of education, psychology of learning, and teaching methods. Aspiring secondary school teachers most often major in the subject they plan to teach while also taking a program of study in teacher preparation. Teacher education programs are now required to include classes in the use of computers and other technologies in order to maintain their accreditation. Most programs require students to perform a student-teaching internship.

Many states now offer professional development schools, which are partnerships between universities and elementary or secondary schools. Students enter these one-year programs after completion of the bachelor's degree. Professional development schools merge theory with practice and allow students to experience a year of teaching firsthand, under professional guidance.

With additional preparation, teachers may move into positions as school librarians, reading specialists, guidance counselors, or instructional coordinators. Teachers may become administrators or supervisors, although the number of these positions is limited, and competition can be intense. In some systems, highly qualified, experienced teachers can become senior or mentor teachers, with higher pay and additional responsibilities. They guide and assist less-experienced teachers while keeping most of their own teaching responsibilities. Preschool teachers usually work their way up from assistant teacher to teacher to lead teacher—who may be responsible for the instruction of several classes—and, finally, to director of the center. Preschool teachers with a bachelor's degree frequently are qualified to teach kindergarten through grade three as well.

Tenure. At the elementary and high school levels, most states have tenure laws that prevent teachers from being fired without just cause and due process. Teachers may obtain tenure after they have satisfactorily completed a probationary period of teaching, normally three years. Tenure does not absolutely guarantee a job, but it does provide some security.

At the college level, attaining tenure is a major step in the traditional academic career. New tenure-track faculty members usually are hired as instructors or assistant professors and must serve a period—usually seven years—under term contracts. At the end of the period, their record of teaching, research, and overall contribution to the institution is reviewed; tenure is granted if the review is favorable. Those denied tenure usually must leave the institution. Tenured professors cannot be fired without just cause and due process. Tenure protects the faculty's academic freedom —the ability to teach and conduct research without fear of being fired for advocating controversial or unpopular ideas. It also gives both faculty and institutions the stability needed for effective research and teaching and provides financial security for faculty. Some institutions have adopted post-tenure review policies to encourage ongoing evaluation of tenured faculty.

The number of tenure-track positions is declining as institutions seek greater flexibility in dealing with financial matters and changing student interests. Institutions rely more heavily on limited-term contracts and part-time, or adjunct, faculty, thus shrinking the total pool of tenured faculty. Limited-term contracts, typically two to five years, may be terminated or extended when they expire, but they generally do not lead to the granting of tenure. In addition, some institutions have limited the percentage of faculty who can be tenured.

For most postsecondary teachers, advancement involves a move into administrative positions, such as departmental chairperson, dean, or president. At four-year institutions, such advancement requires a doctoral degree. At two-year colleges, a doctorate is helpful but not usually required, except for advancement to some top administrative positions.

Working Conditions

Including the school duties that are performed outside the classroom, many teachers work more than forty hours per week. Most work the traditional ten-month school year with a two-month vacation during the summer. Those on the ten-month schedule may teach in summer sessions, take other jobs, travel, or pursue other personal interests. Many enroll in college courses or workshops to fulfill continue education requirements. Teachers in districts with a year-round schedule typically work eight weeks, are then on vacation for one week, and most have a three- to five-week midwinter break.

College faculty members generally have flexible schedules. Usually, they must be present for classes twelve to sixteen hours per week and also for faculty and committee meetings. In addition, most set up regular office hours for students to come to see them whenever necessary. The rest of their time is devoted to preparing for classes, grading papers and exams, conducting research, supervising graduate students, and so forth.

Some teach night and weekend classes. This is particularly true for teachers at two-year community colleges or institutions with large enrollments of older students who have full-time jobs or family responsibilities. Most colleges and universities require teachers to work nine months of the year, which allows them the time to teach additional courses, do research, travel, or pursue nonacademic interests during the summer and school holidays. Colleges and universities usually have funds to support research or other professional development needs of full time faculty, including travel to conferences and research sites.

University faculty may experience a conflict between their responsibilities to teach students and the pressure to do research and publish their findings. This may be a particular problem for young faculty seeking advancement in four-year research universities. Also, recent cutbacks in support workers and the hiring of more part-time faculty have put a greater administrative burden on full-time faculty. Requirements to teach online classes also have added greatly to the workloads of postsecondary teachers. Many find that developing the courses to put online, plus learning how to operate the technology and answering large amounts of e-mail, is very time-consuming.

Salaries

Median annual earnings of kindergarten, elementary, middle, and secondary school teachers ranged from $41,400 to $45,920 in 2004; the lowest 10 percent earned $26,730 to $31,180; the top 10 percent earned $66,240 to $71,370. Median earnings for preschool teachers were $20,980.

According to the American Federation of Teachers, beginning teachers with a bachelor's degree earned an average of $31,704 for the 2003–04 school year. The estimated average salary of all public elementary and secondary school teachers for the 2003–04 school year was $46,597. Private school teachers generally earn less than public school teachers but may be given other benefits, such as free or subsidized housing.

Teachers can boost their salaries in a number of ways. In some schools, teachers receive extra pay for coaching sports and working with students in extracurricular activities. Getting a master's degree or national certification often results in a raise in pay, as does acting as a mentor. Some teachers earn extra income during the summer by teaching summer school or performing other jobs in the school system.

Median annual earnings of all postsecondary teachers in 2005 were $51,800. The middle 50 percent earned between $36,590 and $72,490. The lowest 10 percent earned less than $25,460, and the highest 10 percent earned more than $99,980.

Earnings for college faculty vary according to rank and type of institution, geographic area, and field. According to a 2004–05 survey by the American Association of University Professors, salaries for full-time faculty averaged $68,505. By rank, the average was $91,548 for professors, $65,113 for associate professors, $54,571 for assistant professors, $39,899 for instructors, and $45,647 for lecturers.

Faculty in four-year institutions earn higher salaries, on average, than do those in two-year colleges. In 2004–05, faculty salaries averaged $79,342 in private independent institutions, $66,851 in public institutions, and $61,103 in religiously affiliated private colleges and universities. In fields with high-paying career paths—medicine, law, engineering, and business, among others—earnings exceed these averages. In other fields—such as the humanities and education—they are lower.

Many faculty members have significant earnings in addition to the base salary from consulting, teaching additional courses, research, writing for publication, or other employment. In addition, many college and university faculty enjoy some unique benefits, including access to campus facilities, tuition waivers for dependents, housing and travel allowances, and paid sabbatical leaves. Part-time faculty usually have fewer benefits than full-time faculty.

Earnings for postsecondary career and technical education teachers vary widely by subject, academic credentials, experience, and region of the country. Part-time instructors usually receive few benefits.

The Job Hunt

There are a number of resources that educators can use to help with their job searches.

College Career Placement Centers

Most colleges maintain career centers that receive regular job listings. They are posted on bulletin boards or housed in ring binders. You can also leave your resume on file there. Prospective employers often contact college career offices looking for likely candidates.

The Internet

This is an incredible source of information and particularly helpful to those who are job hunting. Use any of the search engines available to you and type in key words such as *employment*, *teaching*, and *jobs*. The search results will include educational institutions, publications, and a wide variety of potential employers and job search services—most of which are available to you at no charge. Many newspapers also upload their classified sections to the Internet, and you can often examine online the help wanted ads in local newspapers or papers in the geographic location in which you'd prefer to work.

The Direct Approach

Contact school districts in desired areas to find out if they are interested in hiring new staff members. If not, ask that your application be kept on file for future openings.

Newspaper Want Ads

Many school districts advertise the need for educators in newspapers. In particular, check the Sunday classifieds.

The Chronicle of Higher Education

This is the old standby for those seeking positions with two- and four-year colleges and universities. It is a weekly publication available by subscription or in any library or college placement office.

Placement Agencies

For private schools particularly, both at home and abroad, placement agencies can provide a valuable source for finding employment. Some agencies charge both the employer and the future employee a fee; others charge just one or the other.

Words from the Pros

Three professional teachers share their experiences to help you see whether working in education appeals to you.

Michele Lyons Lefkovitz, Elementary Art Teacher

Michele Lyons Lefkovitz is an elementary art teacher at Forest Glen Elementary School in Indianapolis, Indiana. The school is part of an International Magnet Program and serves over seven hundred students in kindergarten through fifth grade. Michele earned her bachelor's and master's degrees in education from the Herron School of Art at Indiana University. She is a Certified Arts and Crafts Teacher for the state of Indiana and has earned a Life License to teach kindergarten through twelfth grades.

Michele's first professional assignment was teaching art to first through sixth graders in at an elementary school, substituting for a teacher who was on maternity leave. After one semester, she moved to another elementary school, where she taught for three and a half years. When her children were born, Michele took a ten-year leave. She returned to teaching in 1990, taking a position as middle school art teacher in Pike Township, Indianapolis. She taught at two middle schools in the district before starting at Forest Glen Elementary, where she has worked for ten years.

Michele says that she became an artist at age four when she got her first box of crayons in kindergarten. "I have always loved the creative process of using the medium of art to express myself," she says. "Paint, crayons, markers, colored pencils, pen and ink, paper, scissors, glue, and pencils have been my companions for all these years. Color is one of my favorite elements of design. From an early age, I was very aware of color and all the many variations of each hue."

When she was ready for college, Michele knew that she wanted to attend art school. She initially considered a career in commercial art and began as a design major. After two quarters, she switched to art education, which combined her love of fine arts with her love of children. "It has been a perfect combination for me," Michele says. "I still enjoy graphic design, and I have been the yearbook advisor for eight years. Teaching art has been extremely rewarding, and I feel very fortunate in my chosen profession."

Michele teaches six forty-five-minute classes a day for a total of thirty classes each week. Each day, she teaches grades five, four, three, two, and then one. In the morning, she is responsible for getting all 750 students to their classrooms; in the afternoon, she makes sure that they get on the correct buses.

Because Forest Glen Elementary is an international school, the curriculum is driven by social studies. Each grade level studies a different continent, and Michele teaches art with a multicultural focus. For example, the first graders learn about Latin America, second graders study Africa and Australia, third graders learn about Asia, fourth graders about Europe, and fifth graders study North America. "Since the world is full of many cultures and art forms," Michele says, "I literally have the world at my fingertips. In my class, we are all individuals from many cultures, and we value diversity. I also make use of my extensive collection of international dolls to teach art forms and cultures."

Michele tries to make the most of the diverse nature of the curriculum by helping her students to express themselves in as many ways as possible. Throughout the year, each child will draw, paint, work with clay, cut paper, and use crayon, marker, chalk, and colored pencils. Older students use ink as well. The topics vary by age and grade, but all share the same mediums. In each session, Michele spends a few minutes giving the class instructions and allows a five-minute cleanup at the end of the period. The rest of the class time is spent creating. Michele describes her days as busy and full and says that she is never bored. She strives to get her students to share her enthusiasm and to experience a sense of freedom and expression in her classroom.

"I love the relationships I have with my students and their families," Michele says. "As an art teacher, I have the same students for all five years of elementary school. So I really get to know them well. I am allowed to see them mature and grow up.

"I would highly recommend the field of art education. However, it's important to know that there are considerably fewer art teachers in a school system than there are regular classroom teachers. In fact, some schools don't even have an art teacher. Thus, the principle of supply and demand comes into play. So I would suggest that perhaps a person have a second area of study as a backup. Most important—I would recommend that you follow your dreams, and if you choose what you love to do, you will be happy."

Louise Tenbrook Whiting, Instructor/Trainer

Louise Tenbrook Whiting earned a master of arts degree in counseling psychology from Sierra University in Santa Monica, California. She is a certified online therapist, life coach, and clinical hypnotherapist. Her specialties include communication skills, assertiveness training, crisis intervention, and counseling for sexual abuse, domestic violence, and chemical dependency.

Louise was a member of a songwriters' organization in southern California and taught music classes. Although she was providing a service, she knew that something was lacking, and she took a job as program manager for a crisis-intervention/suicide-prevention hotline. In addition to managing the office, Louise helped others with problems and found it rewarding to train people to do the same. She decided to return to college and major in counseling psychology. Louise has been involved in teaching and training in communication and interpersonal skills ever since.

Louise enjoys being self-employed and working alone in her home office. "I am in a stress-free environment where I am able to set my own schedule and make changes as desired," She says. "When I have an outside appointment, I simply adjust my schedule. If I choose to work late or in the middle of the night, I have that option. When I decide to take time off, I am able to do so—within reason, of course."

The majority of Louise's teaching is done online. She teaches classes on speaking skills, communication, and interpersonal skills. She uses her education, former employment, and life experience to develop the classes and write the course materials. Most of the classes are self-study.

She also teaches some classes in person, which allows her to interact with students and observe facial expressions and body language. Louise says, "I love to use humor—this works in person yet does not translate well online. I am a performer at heart, and being in front of an audience, students or otherwise, is great!"

What Louise likes the least about teaching in person is that the days are usually long and exhausting. Although she is sometimes initially anxious, she soon finds herself feeling comfortable before the class. Overall, she says the downsides are minimal.

Although she prefers working alone, Louise says that having someone else around tends to create more energy. She also finds that having others around helps to keep her from becoming too isolated and concentrating too heavily on work. Louise's income comes from different sources, which means that her work offers variety. However, this also means her income varies from month to month, and there is frequently a time lapse in receiving it.

Louise has some recommendations for anyone interested in pursing a similar career. She says, "The advice I would give to others is to determine what your interest or your passion is and learn what education or skills you need to acquire before pursuing your dream, then follow through with what you have learned you must do, discipline yourself to achieve your dream (no matter what the challenges are or who tries to dissuade you), and never give up.

"Following a recent class I taught, I received an e-mail from one of the students. Here is a quote from that e-mail: 'You are the first person in my entire thirty years who has ever stood up in front of me and made any sense to me at all. I would not change this day in class for anything. I feel that I learned more from being there than from any other day in my entire life.' This makes the job worth every minute of it."

David Mecozzi, Teacher

David Mecozzi earned his bachelor of science degree in business administration from California State University at Northridge. He earned his teaching credential at the University of Redlands in California. For the past three years he has been employed by the

Etiwanda School District as a sixth grade teacher at Heritage Intermediate School in Fontana, California.

Prior to working at Heritage Intermediate, he spent five years as a fifth grade teacher at West Heritage Elementary School and three years as a sixth grade teacher in San Bernardino. Before teaching, David worked for ten years in the business world. The last five years were with IBM Corporation, and he took one of the company's severance packages to pursue a career in teaching because he wanted a career that would make a difference in society. "I was, and continue to be, concerned about the adult role models our future—the kids—have," David says. "So, instead of just griping about it, I looked into careers that would satisfy that concern. Teaching jumped out at me. Coaching Little League baseball, I believe, made me start thinking that I really wanted to work with children."

David was also attracted to the schedule he would have as a teacher. Since he missed much of his son's infancy due to business trips and long working hours, the idea of a teacher's schedule appealed to him. However, the reality of that schedule was a bit different from what David expected. "Now here's the actual scoop," he says. "I get to work at 7:30 A.M. The kids come into the classroom at 8 A.M. and leave at 2:30 P.M. Between 2:30 P.M. and 4:30 P.M., I clean my room, eat lunch (I work through lunch), grade papers, prepare for the next day, attend grade-level committee meetings, and so forth. By contract, I am obligated to stay until 3 P.M. The time I actually leave is around 4:30 P.M. Since I pick up my own kids from school and the sitter, that is the time I have to leave. And I am not alone; there are teachers who don't leave the school until 6:30 P.M. every day, including Friday. During the heart of the school year, I can be found awake late at night thinking of how to reach the kids or how to present something in a different manner. I rarely get a full night's sleep from September through June."

David explains that a teacher's typical day is extremely hectic due in part to the many interruptions that must be handled. He is responsible for teaching six different subjects and ensuring that his students meet grade-level standards. He has to develop lessons that are engaging enough to interest even those students who don't want to be at school. Teachers also need to deal with paperwork and administrative duties, which many find frustrating and a distraction from actual teaching duties. Dealing with parents is another time-consuming but necessary responsibility that David must deal with, since he must adequately address all concerns and questions about his students and his practices.

David also works hard to create a realistic environment in his classroom. Students often expect teachers to be experts at everything and view their instructors as all-knowing. David spends the first few weeks of each school year working to change that image because he believes it makes a difference when students see that even the teacher makes mistakes. The students feel freer to try and ultimately learn more because they are less worried about being right or wrong.

"To me, the greatest reward of teaching is having a positive effect on a child's life," David says. "I have received several letters from former students who have told me that they are doing well in school because they listened to me. I can't recall one time in the business world that I experienced the warm feeling I felt after reading those letters.

"I enjoy being able to 'perform' in front of kids, and making them laugh brings me much happiness. I enjoy the 'aha' moments when the kids learn something for the first time. I enjoy how the job lets my creativity flow. On the other hand, I am dismayed by children who have little or no motivation to learn and are bent on taking my time away from those students who do. Nothing is more frustrating to a teacher than to watch a child choose not to grow."

David is frustrated by the disrespect he senses toward the teaching profession. In his opinion, many people think that teaching is easy and that anyone can do it. To counteract this, he offers some specific advice to anyone considering a career in teaching:

"One: Get into teaching only if you want to help children develop into successful adults. If you're in it only for the schedule, you won't put in the time required to be an effective teacher. You, the profession, and, most importantly, the kids will suffer.

"Two: Do what's right for the students first, then yourself second. If teaching that social studies lesson would really help the students, even though you'd rather keep on with math—switch to social studies. If sending work folders home weekly makes parents happy, though it's more work for you, do it.

"Three: Find a mentor. It doesn't have to be one assigned to you by your district. Find a helpful person on campus you can go to and talk things over with, commiserate with, and so forth. This helped get me through my first year.

"Four: Never be a reason people say your profession is not really a profession. Dress and act professionally. Treat all with equal respect.

"Five: Never forget that, whether you like it or not, you are a role model. A major part of this job is being a role model. If you don't want to be one, don't enter the profession.

"Six: Never forget that you are not the students' friend; you are their teacher—a far greater role in their lives. If you try to be their friend, you are not only letting your profession down but your students as well.

"Seven: Be consistent and fair. When you make a rule, don't waver. Stick to it. If the students feel it's unfair, listen. If it is, change it. But if it is fair, don't. Remember rule number six on this one. Sometimes you will be very unpopular, but the kids will thank you for it (not all of them, but most will). And, in the long run, you are performing a greater service."

For More Information

Information on teachers' unions and education-related issues may be obtained from:

American Federation of Teachers
555 New Jersey Avenue NW
Washington, DC 20001
www.aft.org

National Education Association
1201 Sixteenth Street NW
Washington, DC 20036
www.nea.org

A list of institutions with teacher education programs accredited by the National Council for Accreditation of Teacher Education can be obtained from:

National Council for Accreditation of Teacher Education
2010 Massachusetts Avenue NW, Suite 500
Washington, DC 20036
www.ncate.org

For information on voluntary teacher certification requirements, contact:

National Board for Professional Teaching Standards
1525 Wilson Boulevard, Suite 500
Arlington, VA 22209
www.nbpts.org

A list of institutions offering training programs in special education may be obtained from:

Council for Exceptional Children
1110 North Glebe Road, Suite 300
Arlington, VA 22201
www.cec.sped.org

For additional information, contact:

American Association for Adult and Continuing Education
10111 Martin Luther King Jr. Highway, Suite 200C
Bowie, MD 20720
www.aaace.org

American Association of Christian Schools
602 Belvoir Avenue
East Ridge, TN 37412
www.aacs.org

American Association of Colleges for Teacher Education
1307 New York Avenue NW, Suite 300
Washington, DC 20005
www.aacte.org

American Association of State Colleges and Universities
1307 New York Avenue NW
Washington, DC 20005
www.aascu.org

Association for Childhood Education International
17904 Georgia Avenue, Suite 215
Olney, MD 20832
www.acei.org

Council for American Private Education
13017 Wisteria Drive, Suite 457
Germantown, MD 20874
www.capenet.org

National Association for the Education of Young Children
1313 L Street NW, Suite 500
Washington, DC 20005
www.naeyc.org

National Association of Independent Schools
1620 L Street NW, Suite 1100
Washington, DC 20036
www.nais.org

About the Author

Jan Goldberg's love for the printed page began well before her second birthday. Regular visits to the book bindery where her grandfather worked produced a magic combination of sights and smells that she carries with her to this day.

Childhood was filled with composing poems and stories, reading books, and playing library. Elementary and high school included an assortment of contributions to school newspapers. While a full-time college student, Goldberg wrote extensively as part of her job responsibilities in the College of Business Administration at Roosevelt University in Chicago. After receiving a degree in elementary education, she was able to extend her love of reading and writing to her students.

Goldberg has written extensively in the occupations area for *Career World* magazine for high school and middle school students, as well as for the many career publications produced by Cass Communications. She has also contributed to a number of projects for educational publishers, including Capstone Publishing, Publications International, Scott Foresman, Addison-Wesley, and Camp Fire Boys and Girls. She is coauthor of the revised and updated edition of *Perfectionism: What's Bad About Being Too Good?*

As a feature writer, Goldberg's work has appeared in *Parenting Magazine, Today's Chicago Woman, Opportunity Magazine, Correspondent, Chicago Parent, Successful Student, Complete Woman, North Shore Magazine,* and the Pioneer Press newspapers. In all, she has published more than 350 pieces as a full-time freelance writer.

In addition to *Careers for Persuasive Types and Others Who Won't Take No for an Answer*, she is the author of *Careers for Class Clowns and Other Engaging Types*, *Careers for Color Connoisseurs and Other Visual Types*, *Careers for Competitive Spirits and Other Peak Performers*, *Careers for Courageous People and Other Adventurous Types*, *Careers for Patriotic Types and Others Who Want to Serve Their Country*, *Careers for Scientific Types and Others with Inquiring Minds*, *Careers in Journalism*, *Great Jobs for Accounting Majors*, *Great Jobs for Computer Science Majors*, *Great Jobs for Music Majors*, *Great Jobs for Theater Majors*, *On the Job: Real People Working in Communications*, *On the Job: Real People Working in Entertainment*, *On the Job: Real People Working in Science*, *Opportunities in Entertainment Careers*, *Opportunities in Horticulture Careers*, and *Opportunities in Research and Development Careers*, all published by McGraw-Hill.